D0049368

THE WEAPONS OF YOUR WARFARE

Equipping Yourself to Defeat the Enemy

LARRY LEA

Creation House
Altamonte Springs, Florida

Creation House
Strang Communications Company
600 Rinehart Road
Lake Mary, FL 32746

Contents

"For though we walk in the flesh, we do not war according to the flesh. For the weapons of our warfare are not carnal but mighty in God for pulling down strongholds, casting down arguments and every high thing that exalts itself against the knowledge of God, bringing every thought into captivity to the obedience of Christ."

—2 Corinthians 10:3-5

"For we do not wrestle against flesh and blood but against principalities, against powers, against the rulers of the darkness of this age, against spiritual hosts of wickedness in the heavenly places."

—Ephesians 6:12

Introduction

The letters I had in my hand reported incidents so disturbing that they burned themselves into my mind. Two reports of similar events in England and New England had first come to my friend C. Peter Wagner, professor at Fuller Theological Seminary in Pasadena, who asked me to read them. Both had been written by outstanding men of God.

One man wrote: "It was brought to our attention that a group of satanists who worshipped in a church within London had committed themselves to pray to Satan for the elimination of a number of our evangelical leaders in the city through marriage and family breakdown....In the course of the previous year they had succeeded through their prayers to Satan in eliminating five of our leading men from pastoral ministries through immorality and marriage breakdown."

The other man wrote: "During the flight from Detroit I had a man sitting next to me who seemed to have little interest in conversation. As we crossed the halfway point in the trip, he bowed his head as though he were praying. After his lips stopped moving and he raised his head, I mentioned positively, 'Are you a Christian?' I had not given him any indication that I was a Christian, a Baptist pastor and a university professor.

"He looked shocked at my question and commented, 'Oh, no. You have me all wrong. I'm not a Christian—I'm actually a satanist.' I asked him what he was praying for as a satanist. He answered, 'Do you really want to know?' When I assured him that I did, he said, 'My primary attention is directed toward the fall of Christian pastors and their families living in New England.' He was serious about his mission."

These two reports confirmed what I have believed as I've traveled the world in calling men and women to prayer:

Satan is loose on the earth.

He is seeking, with a vengeance, whom he may devour.

He is organized.

And he's winning souls and destroying lives this very hour.

"The time," Peter said, "has never been more right for your apostolic ministry of prayer, Larry. We need you to teach the body of Christ how to pray and to inspire us to catch the spirit of militant warfare."

"That's because the enemy has never been more aggressive," I said. And I believe that with all my heart.

Geraldo Rivera, telejournalist and talk-show host, recently featured the growing satanist movement as his topic for a two-hour prime-time special.

As this book goes to press, news reports abound about the terror of gang "wilding" and warfare, even as gangs seek to "franchise" themselves across the nation. Many of these groups have their roots in occult and satanic rituals.

Headlines scream about bodies uncovered just south of the Rio Grande, the victims of satanic ritual.

It isn't fantasy. It isn't a scare tactic. It's real. And it's a matter of life and death for you, your family, your church and your city now and in the future.

If you're not open to the reality of the war in which we're

engaged against Satan and his demons or unwilling to address the possibility of an active evil attacking you and those around you, then this book is not for you. But if you want to fight the enemy, then this manual on spiritual warfare can help equip you for the battle.

As I prayed for you in writing this book, I knew that you must read it and let its message sink deep within your spirit. What is written here is critical to you and your loved ones.

You see, God has no other strategy than you. He has no "Plan B." You're His plan for defeating the devil and his minions on the earth. You must get the truths of this book within you so that you can engage in battle for the Lord, for His honor and for His victory. You must learn how to win the battle and then do it.

Why? For your own sake. God wants you to defeat the devil so you might become all He created you to be in Christ Jesus. You are more than your job or your career or your possessions or even your role in a family. You are a child of the king of kings and Lord of lords, Jesus Christ. That's who you are and why you are a warrior.

And you must win not only for your own sake, but also for your family's sake. Families today are under severe attack: divorce, abuse of all kinds, immorality, extreme poverty and hardship. The family is being assaulted from within and without.

The time is now. Fight so that God's purposes might be accomplished in the earth. God's desire is that none should perish but that all should be saved. That is His heart's cry.

As a believer in Jesus Christ, you are the only one who can push back the forces of darkness, bind the devil's power and give entrance to the Lord Jesus on this earth. Your prayers pave the way for His entry into a sinner's life. Your prayers make it possible for strongholds to be torn down so that captives might be set free. Your prayers tear away the shackles and remove the blindfolds that keep men and women in bondage and darkness. It's up to you, to me, to all of us in the body of Christ to do it.

How? With the weapons of warfare given to us by our Lord Jesus Christ.

Think for a moment how it would be to walk with the Lord Jesus into a large room filled with weapons and to have Him say, "Here is all you need to defeat the devil on the earth—for My sake, for your sake, for your family's sake and for the sake of all who are lost."

I don't know about you, but I know what I'd do. I'd cry out, "Lord, show me how to use these weapons and then show me where the battle is!"

This book is a how-to manual for God's storehouse of spiritual weapons. You'll find in His storehouse all the weapons you need to defeat the devil:

The blood of Jesus—your key to overcoming the devil, to being forgiven, to breaking the devil's hold on your life, to experiencing the presence of the Lord in the midst of your struggles and to being "the righteousness of God." It's your foremost weapon, and you can learn how to use it.

Prayer—your number-one priority for each day as you take on the warrior's mind-set of "set, ready, go."

The whole armor of God—both your defense and your offense in Christ Jesus. When you put on the full armor of God, you put on Jesus. And the devil recognizes Jesus as victor, so he flees both from His presence and from yours.

Praise—your marching song as you anticipate victory and cut through the spiritual clouds of worry, fear and doubt.

Speaking the Word—meditating on the Scriptures until the Word of God becomes part of your being and then speaking out what you believe to be the truth about the situation in Christ Jesus. It's a powerful weapon at your disposal.

The name of Jesus—your badge of authority on this earth.

Perseverance—having a never-quit, endure-to-the-end mind-set, a tenacity to fight until you win.

These are the weapons of the warfare to which God calls you today. No one can do it but you. And the good news is that you can do it.

You can become a mighty warrior in Christ Jesus, no matter who you are in the eyes of men. You can become a mighty warrior in Christ Jesus no matter where you live or where you attend church.

Let me ask you two questions. First, do you love the Lord?

How quickly did your heart leap to say yes! He is your joy, your Savior, your life. The depth and fullness of your affection for Him run without measure, without beginning or end.

Second, do you hate the devil?

I can almost hear you saying, "I dunno. Never thought about it."

And yet to love the Lord and His works is to hate the devil and his works. In fact, the more you love the Lord, the more deeply you hate anything that would detract from Him or attempt to diminish Him in any way.

Now one of the foremost ploys of the devil is to steal from you the Word of God after you hear or read it and before you can plant it deep within your spirit. How many people can't remember by 2:00 p.m. on a Sunday afternoon what their pastor preached that very Sunday morning? Jesus said that these "are the ones by the wayside where the word is sown. And when they hear, Satan comes immediately and takes away the word that was sown in their hearts" (Mark 4:15).

My prayer as you read this book is that the devil will not steal this word from you, but that you will remember it, meditate on it and do it—that you will actually live out these truths on a daily basis.

That's why at the end of almost every chapter you'll find

two requests. First, I'll ask you to "close the door on the devil" by taking some very practical steps in response to the information I've just given you. Second, I'll challenge you to pray and agree with me that a habit of using these weapons of warfare will be established in your life.

It's up to you. You are the one who must "close the door on the devil" when he comes knocking at the entrance to your life. You are the one who must enter into agreement with other believers in the body of Christ that the kingdom of God will be established on the earth, and not the kingdom of the enemy.

Take action! Don't let the devil steal the wisdom of this book from you. With that in mind I want you to do two things right now:

1. Close the door on the devil today. Get up from where you're sitting, walk to the nearest open door and slam it shut. As you do it, say aloud, "Devil, I'm closing the door on you in my life, in my family, in my town and in my nation. You have no authority over my life. You have no place in my life. And from this moment on, every time you come around, you'll have the door slammed in your face."

Stop and do it now! Use this physical action to mark a moment of commitment to yourself and to the Lord. Then come right back so we can pray together.

2. Pray and agree together with me that you will not forget God wants you to fight the devil and win. "In the name of Jesus, I agree with you that the words of this book will be sealed into my life forever. I declare today that I am closing the door on the devil right now. I declare that God's weapons will become my weapons of warfare and that the kingdom of God will be established on the earth as it is in heaven. Lord, I declare that from this moment I will be a warrior for You on the earth. I won't let the devil defeat me, bully me or thwart me. I won't let him invade one inch of Your property, Lord, including my own life and the lives of my loved ones. I praise You for Your goodness to me. I praise You for the victory I know is mine in Christ Jesus. Amen!''

ONE

Warriors!

I stared in amazement at the sea of people before me. Just moments before they'd been sitting in rapt attention, listening silently and calmly as a song had been sung, a testimony given, a need described. Then, within seconds, the entire auditorium of that great church in Seoul, South Korea, was transformed into an awesome generator of God's power.

I had never experienced anything like it: 10,000 voices lifted loudly in prayer, with 10,000 bodies swaying under the intensity of their burden in the Spirit, creating visual waves down from the balconies and across the auditorium. Many of them pounded the air with their fists or grasped at the air as if to pull down unseen barriers or cast away unseen obstacles. And their eyes flowed with tears.

I had chills running up and down my spine. I felt wave after wave of the Spirit flowing through my soul and beyond. And I sensed the presence of God as never before.

There in that huge auditorium, I felt as if I were inside a great turbine of prayer connecting the power of God with the needs of man. "Dear God," I prayed in my spirit, "what warriors these people are in Your kingdom!"

My mind quickly raced fifty miles north to where the

political boundaries had been drawn: North Korea, South Korea. These people have become such warriors, I thought, because they live with the knowledge that their enemy is only a few miles away. No wonder they've learned so well how to assault the powers of darkness.

But the Lord quickly said to me, "The North Koreans aren't their enemies."

I had discussed with Paul Yonggi Cho and others in leadership at his great church in Seoul the relationship between the North Koreans and the South Koreans. I had learned something about the centuries upon centuries of family ties of affection and strength spanning the artificial political border that was established just a few decades ago. The North Koreans were family and friends—not enemies.

The enemy is the communist leadership, I reasoned. And again God said in my spirit, "No, the Korean communist leaders are not their true enemy, either."

"How then, Lord," I prayed, "have these people become such warriors travailing at the gates of heaven? Why do they pray with such urgency, with such energy, with such results?"

As I watched them continue in prayer, minute after minute, hour after hour, through the night hours and into the breaking of the dawn, God spoke His answer: "They have learned to recognize their true enemy. They know the true battle. And they are willing to be My soldiers in winning the true war.

"If only My people in America and every nation around the world would wake to see that they too are in a war. If only they too would recognize their true enemy. They too could become mighty men and women of valor in winning the war and in winning every battle they face as individuals, families and churches."

Today as you hold this book in your hand, that is your challenge.

We're in a war. It's the war of all wars. And it has nothing to do, ultimately, with the arms race, military initiatives, "Star Wars," detente or international relationships with world leaders. Those things are but a temporal and earthly reflection of the true war that's being fought in the heavenlies—the great spiritual battle between God and the devil on the battleground of our souls, with all of eternity hung in the balance.

We face an enemy. He's the enemy of our souls. He has only one plan for our lives, and it's a terrible plan. So we're called today to be soldiers in helping to bring about the final victory. We have a part to play.

God won't do it all by Himself. He's calling us to volunteer for this tour of duty, to become mighty warriors. He wants us to discover how to fight and win the battles we face as we take authority over the enemy. He wants to make us victors until that great day when the heavens open and Jesus returns to establish His rule and reign over the entire earth.

Let me warn you that this book is not for the timid. It's not for those who would rather roll over and play dead. Nor is it for those who would rather be a prisoner of war, trapped in the snares of the enemy.

No, this book is for those who choose to overcome the enemy rather than be overcome by him. It's for those who choose to stand up and fight against the devil who comes to steal, kill and destroy their lives, their families, their businesses, their churches. It's for those who will say, "Yes, I'm ready to enlist today. I'm tired of being trampled by the enemy. I'm tired of losing the battles of life. I'm tired of being overrun and caught off guard at every turn. I'm tired of being wounded again and again."

This book is for those who will cry out from the depths of their being: I'm ready for victory now!

If that's you, my friend, then pack your bags, because you're about to move into higher service for God. You're about to become a part of the "spiritually armed forces" of our Almighty Commander of the hosts of heaven. And your life will never be the same.

TWO

Living in a War Zone

Where do you live? What's your address? Los Angeles? New York? Chicago? Dallas? Miami?

No matter what you answer, I'd have to reply, That's not where the real you lives. That's only where your body lives.

The real you, the spirit and soul within you, has a different address. That address is either the kingdom of God or the kingdom of this world. When we're believers in the Lord Jesus Christ, then "in Him we live and move and have our being," according to the Scriptures (Acts 17:28). We're residents of the kingdom of God. So my spiritual address is:

Larry Lea

Kingdom of God

Nothing can be more important than living in the kingdom of God and having the kingdom in us. Nothing should be a greater priority than seeking the kingdom, finding it, experiencing it, living in it daily. The Bible says it plainly: "Seek first the kingdom of God" (Matt. 6:33).

The kingdom of God is the very nature of the Christian life. But what is the kingdom? How can we recognize the kingdom of God? How do we know if we're living there?

The kingdom of God is simply this: When Jesus becomes

the king of our lives and all that is around us.

I have a strong image in my mind every morning when I pray this line of the Lord's prayer: "Your kingdom come. Your will be done, on earth as it is in heaven." I envision Jesus Christ sitting down, as it were, on the throne of my life. And when Jesus Christ sits on the throne, then the kingdom of God is manifest in my life. Romans 14:17 describes the result as righteousness, peace and joy.

We pray, "Your kingdom come...on earth as it is in heaven." Is there any sorrow in heaven? sickness? broken-heartedness? sin? despair? anything that can steal, kill or destroy us? No!

You may say, That doesn't sound much like my spiritual neighborhood. But that's only because most of us are living on the borders of the kingdom. And borders are usually where the fighting is the heaviest—the war zone.

Do you feel as if you're living in a war zone today? For many people the battle is obvious. They just look out their door, after they've unbolted several locks and unlatched several chains, to see yet other houses with boards across the windows or iron bars across doors or high fences and locked gates. In a land of freedom, many of us are living in fear of drug lords, gangs and criminals intent on robbery and murder.

Much of the war around us is less visible but no less real. It happens behind those locked doors: abuse of all kinds; drunkenness; anger; hatred; deceit; perversion; broken relationships; raped emotions.

No matter where you look in the physical realm, a deadly war is raging. But even as bad as it is, it's still not the *real* war.

The real war is eternally deadly—the war behind the war. And if you're living spiritually on the fringes of the kingdom of God, you'll be subject to its most intense battles.

Entering the Fullness of God's Kingdom

Compare two verses of Scripture, both of which are the words of Jesus: "Do not fear, little flock, for it is your Father's good pleasure to give you the kingdom" (Luke 12:32). "And from the days of John the Baptist until now the kingdom of heaven suffers violence, and the violent take it by force" (Matt. 11:12).

On one hand, Jesus says that God wants to give us the kingdom. On the other, Jesus says the kingdom of God will be taken by force. How is it that God wants to give us the kingdom, yet we must take it by force?

The reason for the seeming paradox is this: Someone wants to keep us from receiving and experiencing the very thing that God wants to give us.

We know this someone is a thief. The apostle John describes him as one who comes to steal, kill and destroy (John 10:10). We know he is an adversary (1 Pet. 5:8) who walks about as a roaring lion, seeking whom he may devour. He is Satan, the devil, the devourer. Because of Satan, we must become the violent ones who take the kingdom by force if we are ever to receive the very thing that God wants us to have.

We should consider carefully the time we live in, a time not unlike the days of John the Baptist. John lived between two dispensations—the dispensation of law and the dispensation of grace. Today the church is also crouched between two dispensations—the dispensation of grace and the dispensation of the millennial reign of Jesus Christ. We're inching right up to eternity.

Satan has only a little time left. So he's unleashing all of his anger, his evil, his fury upon the world. And because he's the great deceiver, the greatest trick he's playing upon the American church today is the lie that "everything is all right. Everything will come out in the wash. We don't have anything to worry about. Get comfortable, enjoy life, and everything will turn out OK."

Despite such lies, you can be assured of one thing today: Satan hates you and has a terrible plan for your life.

God is calling His church to awake. If we are to be the church triumphant, we must become the church militant in this hour. God has freely given us the kingdom, but because we face an intervening enemy, we will have to take our rightful entry into the kingdom by force.

When we pray, "Your kingdom come...on earth as it is in heaven," we're praying that the kingdom of heaven will enter into us here on the earth. We're praying that Jesus will be enthroned as king of our hearts and will establish His reign of righteousness, peace and joy.

At the same time, we're coming against the enemy and against his sin, sickness and sorrow. There's no sin in heaven, so there's no sin in us when Jesus enters as king of our lives to establish His righteousness there. There's no dis-ease in heaven—no heart trouble, either physical or emotional; so there's nothing that would divide our lives and cause us to be in disharmony when Jesus enters as king to establish His peace there. There's no unhappiness in heaven, so there's no depression or sorrow or unhappiness in our lives when Jesus enters as king to establish His joy there.

We Stand Between D-Day and Victory

During World War II the Allies stormed the beaches of Normandy in France on June 6, 1944—now known as D-Day. That battle was the definitive turning point of the conflict; for all practical purposes, the Allies won World War II on that day.

Even so the Germans and Japanese did not sign the documents to surrender officially until the next year. Meanwhile, that one year between D-Day and victory was the bloodiest year in the entire war! More people died during that year than in any other year. The enemy forces knew they only had a little time left and that if they were to claim anything at all they needed to act immediately and powerfully.

The church today stands between its own D-Day and victory. When Jesus Christ was crucified on the cross for the sins of mankind, that was D-Day; technically, Satan was defeated. But until Jesus comes again in victory to establish His kingdom officially and to force Satan to surrender all authority to Him, the church is engaged in the final throes of the war. So we're experiencing intense opposition and some of the "bloodiest" fighting of all time, spiritually speaking.

If you think the church isn't under seige by an enemy, then visit the hospitals for a day or sit in my office and answer the telephone calls. As a minister of the gospel, I see or speak to hundreds of people each week who are broken in their hearts, bodies, minds and homes.

Let this fact sink into your mind today: Satan is running rampant, looking for his opportunity to nail you. He is not just *the* adversary; he is *your* adversary. He is not just *the* enemy; he is *your* enemy. He is not just *the* liar and thief; he is the one who is lying to *you*, telling *you* that everything will be fine if you just lay low and don't do anything to rock the boat. He is the thief who is ripping *you* off. He is the one who comes to destroy *you*.

We must break through the enemy ranks to give Jesus reign over every aspect of our lives: our minds, emotions and bodies; our finances, jobs and businesses; our homes, marriages and families. And in order for Him to establish His righteousness, peace and joy there, we must develop the mentality of a warrior.

A Warrior's Mentality

Are you trying just to "get through" this life, just to "get by"? If so, you need to take a look at the standard of the

New Testament. The New Testament standard is not to "get through," but to *win*.

I like what Snoopy said in one of the Peanuts cartoons by Charles Schultz: "It doesn't matter whether you win or lose—until you lose." Many people think that to be a Christian means just to get by, and if you lose or get beat up or trampled in the process, that's just the way life is. But that kind of passive attitude is not the Christian viewpoint. Those who lose, as Snoopy observed, come to realize instead that winning *does* matter.

The Christian viewpoint is that we won't only run this race; we'll win! We are to run in order that we might obtain (1 Cor. 9:24)—in other words, we're to give it all we've got! We're to run as if we're going for the gold medal.

When my son was just seven years old, I went into his room one evening to lay my hands on him and pray for him—which has been our custom for all our children since they were born. As he lay in his bunk bed, he pulled me down close and said, "Daddy, I know something about you."

"OK," I said, "what is it? What do you know about me?"

"I know you're not the greatest preacher in the whole world."

"Well, son, I know that, too. That's true."

"But I want to tell you something else I know about you, Dad."

By now I was getting a little concerned about what he thought he knew about me, but I asked, "And what is that?"

He answered, "I believe you may be the greatest warrior in the whole world."

I could not have received a higher compliment from anyone. I may not be the greatest preacher in the world. I may not be the greatest anything. But I pray, "Lord, let me be a great warrior in the army You're raising up today!"

If I awoke late one night to the screams of my little girls and discovered an intruder in their room, you would see me turn into an awesome fighting machine. Nothing about me would be calm, cool or collected. That's the same way I feel about what Satan is doing today. We must determine in our hearts that we won't sit by and take it any more.

Some people simply view the enemy's attack as a fact to be accepted: "Oh, she's sick and that's just the way it is." "They're having trouble in their family and it will probably end in divorce. That's just part of life." "Times are tough and bankruptcy is just a fact of our society."

When I hear statements like these, everything in me cries out, "No!" That isn't just the way it is—in God's eyes. It's a lie of the enemy that bad things must happen to God's people because "that's just the way it is in life." Too many bad things are happening because God's people are *allowing* them to happen. They aren't standing up to say, "I have a warrior's mentality and I'm determined to see the kingdom of God established in my life. I'm determined to fight with all my might against the enemy. I'm determined to win this battle and ultimately the war."

Do you want to lose a fight? Get hit and then start backing up. You'll get hit again.

Do you want to win a fight? Then no matter how hard you're hit, stand firm, swing back and keep swinging. Plant your feet as if in concrete, and get your arms swinging as fast as you can make them go. Then watch what happens!

Fighting in the spirit realm works the same way. Get hit and back up, and you'll get hit again. Get hit and resist, and you'll send the enemy fleeing.

We must learn where we stand and how to stand. We must know who we are and where we are if we're to win this war. So we must begin by knowing more about the enemy and his limitations—what I call spiritual reconnaissance.

Close the Door on the Devil Today

1) Write your name below to declare your "permanent address" here and now as a lasting reminder of your commitment to live in the kingdom of God.

My permanent address is

Zabella Diamond   3.01.90

(Your name here)
Kingdom of God

2) Determine today that you *will* seek first the kingdom of God and that you *will* experience the fullness of His righteousness, peace and joy in your life. Say aloud right now: "Devil, I won't be defeated. I will experience the kingdom of God. I will resist you with all that I have and all that I am."

Pray With Me

Let's agree together you'll never forget that the kingdom of God is your first priority: "In the name of Jesus, I agree with you that this word is sealed forever in my heart. I declare today that I am a child of God and I live in the kingdom of God. I declare that Jesus is the Lord of lords and king of kings in my life. I declare that I will take a stand against the devil in every area of my life and that from this day forward I will have a warrior's mentality. I will *not* take loss as a final answer to any circumstance in my life. In the name of Jesus, Amen."

THREE

Reconnaissance: Recognizing Your Enemy

How big is the devil to you? Is he as big as God? Get honest with yourself. In the everyday, nitty-gritty matters of life, who seems to have more power?

If you're like most people I know—including most Christians I know—you'll say with your head, and even with your heart, that God is bigger than the devil. But do your actions, and does that feeling in the pit of your stomach, line up with your head and heart?

Most people I know give the devil far more credit than he's due. They don't really understand the relationship between God and the devil. They cry, "I'm no match for the devil. He's too big for me. He's too strong. He's too powerful. He's too—too—too—too...."

Of course, that's true if you're not a believer in the Lord Jesus Christ. If you're still living in your sins and have never experienced the forgiveness of Jesus in your life, then you're fighting an enemy who is bigger than you are.

But if you're a believer in the Lord Jesus Christ, this is what my Bible says about your situation: "He who is in you is greater than he who is in the world" (1 John 4:4). When we apply that truth personally, we can say with confidence: He who is in me (Jesus) is greater than he who is in this world (the devil).

Your Enemy Is Limited

God and the devil are not on equal planes trying to fight out the battle for your soul. Many people picture in their mind's eye that God is on one side and the devil on the other, while they themselves are somewhere in the middle being pulled in one direction or the other. They usually picture the playing field as level. But that isn't at all the case.

God is omnipresent. He is everywhere at the same time, while the devil is limited in time and space. God is also omnipotent; He does whatever He wants to do. But the devil is not all-powerful. He must operate under the rules set out for him by Someone who does have it all under control. The devil can only operate within the parameters that the body of Christ gives to him.

That's a critical point for you to understand today. The devil only has the opportunity to operate where you give him a place to operate. That's why the apostle Paul said, "Do not give place to the devil" (Eph. 4:27). In other words, "Don't offer the devil any space in your life. Don't hang out the 'for rent' sign in any area of your life." If you do, he'll take over that territory every time.

When you have the power of God in your life, when you have Jesus ruling and reigning on the throne of your heart, then He who is in you is greater than he who is in the world. There are, in fact, at least seven things the devil cannot do.

1. The devil cannot penetrate the blood of Jesus.

Several years ago I received a phone call. A man had locked himself in a hotel room and then sent word that he would kill himself unless Larry Lea came and talked to him personally. So I agreed to see him, and Pastor Sonny Conatser went with me.

As we approached the room where the man was supposed to be, we knocked on the door. No answer. We finally tried the door and it was open, so we cautiously walked in. No one was in the room.

I went toward the bathroom, still very cautiously, and by then, all sorts of images were going through my mind. What was I going to find behind that door?

When I opened the bathroom door I found that the shower curtain was pulled shut over the bathtub. When I reached over to pull it back, I heard the door behind me slam loudly.

I turned around to find myself face-to-face with a man who looked just as I had imagined somebody named "Dirty Harry" would look. The man standing just a couple of feet from me in that small bathroom space was about six feet, four inches tall. He had a beard, and in his left hand he was holding a six-pack of beer. I could tell by the look in his eyes that he was high on something more than alcohol.

The man quickly opened his shirt and pulled out a .357 magnum revolver, which he proceeded to point in my direction. Then he glared right into my face and said, "None of us will leave this room alive today." Again and again he repeated that threat, as if he had only one idea and that was it.

Needless to say, in that kind of situation you find out quickly just what kind of faith you have. I began instinctively to plead the blood of Jesus, to claim the power of the blood of Jesus in that situation, and to appropriate the blood of Jesus over my life, Sonny's life and this man's life. Even as this man was ranting and raving incoherently and declaring to me that I would not leave the room alive, I began under my breath to say, "The blood of Jesus covers me. The blood of Jesus has broken the power of the devil. The blood of Jesus protects me. The blood of Jesus covers Sonny."

Why say that? Because the number-one thing the devil cannot do is to penetrate the blood of Jesus Christ. The blood of Jesus has already broken the power of the devil and it is a force, a power, an entity in this universe available to every child of God for deliverance and salvation from every situation, circumstance or sin.

This man didn't know what I was doing or saying. He had no idea what was going on. But suddenly he stopped talking and stared at me, still pointing the pistol at me, as if waiting for my response.

I thought, God, Your Word had better be in my mouth right now. I had no idea what I should or would say. But I believed that the Holy Spirit was in me and that He would speak through me.

I said something and to this day I don't know what it was. My mouth seemed to be speaking words without my mind's involvement. Whatever it was that I said, the next thing I knew the man dropped the revolver down to his side and asked, "Well, what do you want me to do?"

I looked back at him and said, "The first thing I want you to do is to lie down right there on the bed." I have no idea why I said that. I repeated, "Lie down there on the bed!"

He walked over and laid down on the bed, still holding the pistol. I thought, Now what do I do?

I said, "I'm going to pray for you right now." Then I started to pray, "In the name of Jesus, I bind the powers of suicide; I bind the powers of death; I bind the powers of destruction." When I said that, his hand relaxed off the pistol.

I looked at Sonny and said, "Get it!" Sonny wasted no time in getting it. But the man didn't move a muscle; he just lay there.

Then I led the man in the sinner's prayer and he accepted Jesus Christ into his life as his personal Savior and Lord in that hour. What had started out to be a death hour turned into a life hour. What started as a time when the devils were laughing turned into an hour when the angels were rejoicing.

How did this happen? I am firmly convinced it happened because the blood of Jesus was applied at that moment.

Do you remember the first Passover in the book of Exodus when the death angel was sent by God throughout the land of Egypt to destroy the firstborn of every living thing? (See Exodus 14.) The only place that the death angel couldn't go was into those homes where the blood had been applied to the doorposts. That kind of protection is ours today: The devil cannot penetrate where the blood of Jesus is applied.

Every day I apply the blood of Jesus. I say, "The blood of Jesus is over my entire being. The blood of Jesus is over my wife and children. The blood of Jesus is over my home. The blood of Jesus is over my work. The blood of Jesus is over my church."

I let the words of Revelation 12:11 ring in my ears and my heart: "And they overcame him [the accuser, which is the devil himself] by the *blood of the Lamb* and by the word of their testimony." Praise God for the blood of the Lamb and its power in our lives!

2. The devil cannot harm you if you put on the whole armor of God every day and claim your authority in Jesus Christ.

The Bible clearly tells us in Ephesians 6:10-11 to be "strong in the Lord, and in the power of His might." It says that when we put on the whole armor of God we'll be in a position to "stand against the wiles of the devil."

You would never think about leaving your house for a day's work or going to church without putting on your clothes. Neither should we think about leaving our homes in the morning without putting on our spiritual clothes: the truth girding our loins; the breastplate of righteousness covering our hearts; the preparation of the gospel of peace on our feet; the helmet of salvation on our head; the shield of faith and the sword of the spirit in our hands. Fully clothed in this armor, we're able to stand tall in prayer against the powers of darkness. (See Eph. 6:10-18.)

Only when we're dressed in the armor of God this way are we in a position to claim Luke 10:19 for our lives: "Behold, I give you the authority to trample on serpents and scorpions, and over all the power of the enemy, and nothing shall by any means hurt you."

That's the promise of God. But I believe it's the promise of God only to those who choose to have that authority and power in their lives by first putting on the armor of God and by declaring, "Unrighteousness will not rule me; lies will not rule me; fear will not rule me; doubt will not rule me; evil imaginations will not rule me; the lust of the flesh, the lust of the eyes and the pride of life will not rule me."

Then, when the fiery darts of this life come at us, we declare with the word of our faith in God that we will speak blessing instead of cursing, words of faith instead of words of doubt, affirmations about Jesus instead of skepticism. We declare in all circumstances that "God is working all things together for my good" (see Rom. 8:28).

3. The devil cannot read your mind.

We have said that God is omnipresent and omnipotent—that He is everywhere and can do anything. We must realize as well that God is omniscient. He knows everything. But the devil is limited in what he knows. He knows what you say.

Satan cannot read your mind. But he knows your words. So watch what you say. I believe that's the meaning of Hebrews 13:15, which says, "Let us continually offer the sacrifice of praise to God, that is, the fruit of our lips giving thanks to His name."

What are we to speak out? Praise to God for what He is doing in our lives. Thanks to His name for what He has done for us. When? Continually—which means all the time.

There's a good reason for this. It's not so we can be happy-go-lucky Christians, walking around all the time with a glazed look in our eyes and a silly grin on our faces. God doesn't say this to us so we can avoid confronting the reality of life. He says this to us so we can face life head-on and emerge victorious.

God wants us to walk in continual praise and a continual attitude of gratitude because God knows and the devil knows that the spirit realm operates through our words. The Bible says that if you will confess with your mouth the Lord Jesus and believe in your heart that God raised Him from the dead, you will be saved. For with the heart man believes unto righteousness and with the mouth confession is made unto salvation (see Rom. 10:8-9). In other words, your salvation and my salvation are based on a two-step process: first, we believe in our hearts, and second, we confess with our mouths what we believe in our hearts.

I'm not talking about what I would call idle "confessionism"—the belief that whatever you want, you just speak it out and you'll get it. I'm talking about a biblical confession of the Word of God.

When you have faith in your heart that Jesus will win in a situation, that Jesus will be victor, that you are on the side of Jesus, and that the devil will be defeated; when you speak that faith out in the form of praise to God and thanksgiving for what He has already done in your life, then the angelic hosts are released to minister to you as an heir of salvation.

On the other hand, if in your heart you believe that Jesus will not win, that the devil is stronger, and that nothing you do is going to matter; if you speak out that attitude in the form of doubt, discouragement or fear, then the demonic forces have the ability to move into that area of your life to destroy you.

What comes out of your mouth not only activates God in His arena, but it also activates the devil in his arena. That's one reason I say so often, "Pray it before you say it!"

Just about the time you're ready to blurt out a judgment

on a matter, or express some doubt or disgust, or speak out some other un-faith-filled word, stop to ask yourself, Do I even need to say that? Ask God to give you instead a "word of testimony" about Him and about what He can do in the situation. He'll do it! Then the second part of Revelation 12:11 will come to bear: "And they overcame him by the blood of the Lamb and *by the word of their testimony.*"

4. The devil won't leave unless you cast him out.

The Pharisees once confronted Jesus with the accusation that He cast out demons by the name and power of Beelzebub, the prince of demons. (See Matthew 12, beginning with verse 25.) In other words, they were saying that Jesus Himself was demon-possessed and that His miracles were done by the power of Satan working in His life.

Jesus responded to them by saying, "A house divided against itself cannot stand, and if Satan casts out Satan, then his house will fall." He went on to say that if someone wants to steal something from a strong man's house, then he must first come in and bind the strong man. The major point of His response was this: "Satan won't cast out Satan."

A great deal has been said in recent months on the national media networks about satanism and the power of the devil over people's lives. I've been a bit amused that God used the secular media to wake up the church and say, "Hey, guys, the Bible's true."

We had debates when I was in seminary as to whether demons were active in America. We debated whether anyone, and if so, who, had the power to cast out demons if they did exist. Everything was kept theoretical; the fact was totally ignored that even as we discussed the situation, demons of doubt, demons of unbelief, demons of skepticism and demons of mockery were hanging off many people who were roaming the halls of the church.

Now, however, people aren't asking whether demons are real—they're asking what to do about the problem. It's one thing to analyze the situation, but it's another thing altogether to know how to solve it. If our nation is to survive the coming years, I believe it's critical that a group of people be raised up within the church who not only are capable of recognizing the demonic nature of many situations, but who know what to do about demons when they encounter them. And one of the most important realities we need to know as we prepare to tear down spiritual strongholds is that a demon will not destroy itself or give up its territory voluntarily.

It's up to us—to you and to me—to fight the devil. It's up to us to cast him out of the territory he presently holds. It's up to us to resist the devil. First Peter 5:8-9 says, *"Your adversary the devil walks about like a roaring lion, seeking whom he may devour. Resist him!"* (italics added).

A young man from MacAlester, Oklahoma, was recently interviewed on one of the television network talk shows. At the time of his interview, he was sitting on death row. He had fallen into Satan worship as a teenager and the devil had so possessed him that he had lost all conscious control over his own actions. He had brutally murdered his father and mother while in that state of spiritual bondage.

After he'd gone to prison, however, this young man had been born again, delivered from all demonic influence and filled with the Holy Spirit. On the show he was asked about satanism, and even as he sat in prison, awaiting execution, his warning was strong. He insisted that we'd better wake up in our dealing with demons to realize that we cannot counsel or psychoanalyze a demon, because they'll lie to us every time.

That young man knew what he was talking about. You can't "talk" a person out of being possessed by the devil. You can't "convince" a devil to leave voluntarily. They don't leave a stronghold peacefully. They must be cast out. So it's up to men and women of God to take authority over them and to bind their power—and that means you and me.

33

I'll never forget the time I came into a room where a group of people was arguing with a man who was demon-possessed. One of the men finally grabbed the demon-possessed person and shouted angrily, "Tell me the truth, you lying devil!"

That's impossible! How can a liar tell you the truth? The best action would have been to appropriate the blood of Jesus, to speak out the words of faith about the authority and power of Jesus Christ, and cast that demon out of the person's life in the name of Jesus.

5. Satan cannot stop your mountain of need from moving, if you'll sow your seed and speak to that mountain.

We must get it clearly fixed in our minds that the devil cannot stop a miracle from happening which God intends for us. I hear many people say, "Well, the devil did this" or "the devil did that." They give the devil too much credit.

The Bible says, "Do not be deceived, God is not mocked; for whatever a man sows, that he will also reap" (Gal. 6:7). Whatever you have sown, you will reap. No ifs, ands, buts or maybe sos. The problem isn't so much what the devil is doing as it is that people aren't sowing the right kinds of seeds. A weed will only grow where a good plant hasn't already been sown.

Jesus said, "If you have faith as a mustard seed, you will say to this mountain, 'Move from here to there,' and it will move; and nothing will be impossible for you" (Matt. 17:20). The problem doesn't lie solely with the devil. It lies with people who don't have faith; who don't sow that seed of their faith in the right place at the right time, led by the Holy Spirit; who don't say to their mountains of need, "Go!"

Jesus said the mountain will move. He said nothing will be impossible for you. Is your mentality one that says everything is impossible—or that nothing is impossible? Is your mentality one that says, "There's nothing I can do to stop the devil"? Or are you planting your seeds of faith, believing in your heart that God is with you, and then speaking to your need, "Get out of my life, in the name of Jesus"?

The sixth chapter of Galatians goes on to say, "For he that sows to his flesh will of the flesh reap corruption, but he who sows to the Spirit will of the Spirit reap everlasting life. And let us not grow weary while doing good, for in due season we shall reap if we do not lose heart" (Gal. 6:8-9).

That says to me, "Sow and keep sowing. Keep believing. Keep speaking out words of faith—right up to the second when your miracle happens."

I believe there's usually a time interval between the moment you plant your seed and the time your mountain moves. There's a time interval between the planting of any seed and harvest, and it's during that time that your faith will be tested. You'll wonder if your seed will ever come up and produce a harvest. You'll wonder if your mountain really will be moved and cast into the sea. You'll wonder when the due season will come. But the Bible says that if you don't faint—in other words, if you don't give up— then the harvest surely will arrive, the mountain surely will move and victory surely will be yours.

No ifs, ands, buts or maybe sos. The devil can't do anything to keep that victory from happening.

6. The devil cannot stop God's ultimate purposes on the earth from coming to pass.

What are some of God's purposes that the devil cannot stop, slow down or stall? First, the devil cannot stop the church from prevailing. As long as the church stays in prayer and obedience before the throne of God, no matter what hits it, no matter what struggle it faces, no matter what mistakes a person might make (including a pastor), the church will prevail. One of God's supreme purposes is to have a church that is triumphant.

Jesus said, "On this rock I will build my church, and the gates of Hades shall not prevail against it" (Matt. 16:18).

What was that rock? The rock was a declaration of faith that Jesus is the Christ, the Son of the living God. A church that is declaring Jesus to be the Christ, the Son of the living God, is therefore a church that will win.

Years ago in Dallas a local church group was beginning to experience a great move of God among its people. Folks were getting healed and saved, and the church began to grow. Then the pastor of that church got a telephone call.

The person on the other end of the line said, "Now, listen—if you don't stop all that business of preaching that Jesus can heal and deliver people, we're going to kick you out of town." So the pastor said to himself, "Well, I guess I'd better cool it off a little bit."

He did, and the Holy Spirit was grieved. That church began to die, and it eventually ceased to exist.

But do you know what happened at the same time? Brother Howard Conatser, pastor of Beverly Hills Baptist Church, walked out one Sunday morning and said, "Folks, we're just going to worship God today. Let's throw away our bulletin and just let Jesus be Lord of His church." And then he began to pray, "We don't even know how to have church; we don't even know what church is, Lord; but here we are and we are giving ourselves to You."

Do you know what happened? The glory of God fell on that place and people began to worship. The people were in church for three or four hours that morning and nobody cared. Mrs. Barryman, the wife of the chairman of the board of deacons, was healed; God began to convict people; and lives were changed. That church grew from four hundred in Sunday school to more than four thousand people nearly overnight.

Why? Because God is looking for only one thing: an obedient people who will say, "We want only what You want, God." That's all. And when God finds such a person, or such a group of people, that's where He makes His purposes known.

Nothing the devil can do is sufficient to stop the purpose of God from being manifest in power and authority in such an individual or body of believers. The devil can do absolutely nothing to stop God's church from prevailing if it will stay in prayer and obedience and declare that Jesus is the Christ, the Son of the living God.

The second purpose of God that the devil cannot stop is Jesus' coming again. When God almighty looks at His Son, Jesus, and says, "It's time, Son," there will be nothing the devil can do to keep Jesus from returning. The micromillisecond that God wants Jesus to come, He'll come.

I believe we can hasten that day. If we get our work done and do it right, if we take the baton and run with it, I believe we can speed up that process. Jesus is coming for a bride, a church, that stands as a queen, fully clothed in majesty, beauty, holiness and purity. If we will set ourselves about the task of getting ready to be that kind of bride—which is our work and our responsibility—then I believe we can hasten the return of the Lord Jesus Christ.

On the other hand, if we choose not to be Christ's bride; not to get ourselves ready to stand before Him in majesty, beauty, holiness and purity; and not to take up our cross and do His work, then we can stall His return. Either way, however, the coming of the Lord Jesus is not hurried or stalled by anything that Satan does or doesn't do. He is not a factor in the timetable of God.

Third, the devil cannot stop Jesus from casting him into the bottomless pit. When Jesus comes again and says, "Satan, I'm locking you in a bottomless pit," there's nothing Satan can do to keep that from happening. And the same principle holds true in your life. When Jesus casts Satan out of an area of your life, there's nothing Satan can do except go.

In fact, Satan cannot stop any of God's ultimate purposes in you, just as he can't stop God's ultimate purposes for the church or the world or himself. If you're a child of God, then you're immune to death in this life until your purpose is finished. Satan cannot take you out prematurely.

I've talked to many people who fear they will die before they get their work for the Lord accomplished, and that fear has them bound. But I tell you with all the authority of the name of Jesus that you will not leave your physical body where you reside right now—to go to be with the Lord in your spiritual body—until God's purpose is finished in you on this earth. "He who calls you is faithful, who also will do it" (1 Thess. 5:24). What will God do? He will keep your "whole spirit, soul and body...preserved blameless at the coming of our Lord Jesus Christ" (1 Thess. 5:23). Praise God for His faithfulness to us!

7. *The devil cannot confess that Jesus Christ has come in the flesh or that Jesus Christ is Lord.*

The devil will never praise Jesus. He will not declare that the Son of God has come to the earth in the form of a man. He will not proclaim the resurrection of Jesus. He will not declare that Jesus is the Christ or that Jesus is Lord.

The same is true for human beings under the influence of demons. The Bible says that "no one speaking by the Spirit of God calls Jesus accursed, and no one can say that Jesus is the Lord except by the Holy Spirit" (1 Cor. 12:3). Scripture also says, "Every spirit that confesses that Jesus Christ has come in the flesh is of God, and every spirit that does not confess that Jesus Christ has come in the flesh is not of God" (1 John 4:2-3).

Recently in one of our services a young man cried out uncontrollably as we gave the invitation to receive Christ. We quickly discerned that he was filled with a spirit of anger. His was an anger beyond any normal human anger; it was demonically inspired.

As he cried out, I commanded that spirit in him to be quiet in the name of Jesus. Then I commanded it to come out of him. Next I immediately took a third step. I said to the young man, "Now I want you to begin to confess that

Jesus is come in the flesh, that Jesus is the Christ, that Jesus is Lord, that Jesus is setting you free and that Jesus is the Lord of *your* life.'' He did, and the power of God filled his being. He was delivered that night from bondage and was gloriously saved.

We often hear about the "litmus test" for this or that. The scientific litmus test is one designed to tell whether something is alkaline or acid. But there's a "spiritual litmus test" that we can always use to tell whether someone is of God or not. It's this: Does the person confess that Jesus is God's Son come in the flesh and that Jesus is Lord?

If they can sincerely and honestly confess with the full conviction of their spirits that Jesus is God's Son come in the flesh and Jesus is Lord, then they are of God. If they hem and haw around, if they start to make excuses or to qualify their answer, or if they refuse to answer, then their confession is not of God. It's that simple.

A demon won't even say the words "Jesus is Lord" unless it's with a mocking tone of voice. The demons will not confess that Jesus is God's Son come in the flesh. They will not declare Jesus to be Lord.

But we can. It's up to us to declare the lordship of Jesus. In doing so, we bind unbelief and preach the gospel in a way that is truly effective.

To sum up, then, the seven things that the devil cannot do:

1. The devil cannot penetrate the blood of Jesus. Therefore we must be covered by the blood. In the next chapter we'll see how we fully appropriate the blood of Jesus.

2. The devil cannot harm you if you will put on the whole armor of God every day and claim your authority in Jesus Christ. How do we do that? We'll be "Putting on the Uniform" or the armor of God in chapter 6.

3. The devil cannot know all your thoughts. It's up to us to have a Bible-based confession as our "word of testimony" so that when the devil overhears us talking, he only hears the praise of God and thanksgiving for God's presence in our lives. How do we develop a "word of testimony" with which to defeat the devil? We'll explore that in chapter 8 as we learn "Our Battle Cry" as God's soldiers.

4. The devil will not cast himself out. That's our job!

5. The devil cannot stop your miracle from coming when you sow your seeds of faith and then speak to your mountain of need. What you sow is what you will reap. Today is the day for sowing into the kingdom of God.

6. The devil cannot stop God's ultimate purposes in the earth from coming to pass. In the life of the church and in your life, the purposes of God will be established if you'll stay in prayer and obedience and declare that Jesus is the Christ, the Son of the Living God.

7. The devil cannot confess that Jesus Christ has come in the flesh or that Jesus Christ is Lord. That's up to us.

Now why have we spent so much time at the beginning of this book talking about the devil? Because you need a clear picture of your enemy. Knowing who your enemy is and isn't, what he can and cannot do, and how he operates is a critical part of defeating him.

By no means, however, am I attempting to underestimate the devil's power. Those statements I've just given you tell you what the devil cannot do, but if you read them again closely you see some of what the devil can do:

1. The devil cannot penetrate the blood of Jesus. But he can go every place the blood has not been applied. It's up to us to appropriate the blood of Jesus to specific situations and circumstances. When we don't, the devil can hold court.

2. The devil cannot harm you if you put on the whole armor of God every day and claim your authority in Jesus Christ. But if you don't put on the whole armor of God every day, you're a sitting duck.

3. The devil cannot know all your thoughts. But he can know what you say. Your words can give him the entry he needs to work evil. You can put out the welcome mat for him by what you say. His evil work will not only infect your life but the lives of those who hear what you say and take those words into their hearts.

4. The devil will not cast himself out. But wherever he is right now, he'll stay put unless you or someone else comes in the name of Jesus to remove him. Evil isn't going to diminish of its own accord. Whatever territory is claimed by the devil right this minute will stay claimed by the devil unless we act against it.

5. The devil cannot stop your miracle from happening when you sow your seeds of faith and then speak to your mountain of need. But if you aren't sowing seeds of faith, and if in your faith you aren't speaking out against your mountain of need, then you're not in a position to expect miracles from God's hand. The devil can't stop a miracle that God ordains. But he can plant a seed of doubt, fear, unbelief or bitterness that will grow into a "weed" in your life if you fail to plant seeds of faith.

6. The devil cannot stop God's ultimate purposes in the earth from coming to pass. But he will work as hard as he can between his D-Day and victory in your life, in the life of the church and in the history of this earth. He will steal, kill and destroy anything that's not hastening the return of the Lord through prayer, obedience and a declaration that Jesus is the Christ, the Son of the Living God.

7. The devil cannot confess that Jesus Christ has come in the flesh or that Jesus Christ is Lord. But when we don't confess that Jesus Christ is come and that Jesus Christ is Lord, we leave room for the devil to promote his lies. A failure to voice the truth in a situation leaves the door wide open for lies to spread.

Are you getting the picture? Our enemy is mortally wounded and ultimately defeated, but today, right now, in your life and in mine, he's active. He's building strongholds of lies, doubt, deceit and terror. He's causing sickness of every form—not only physical sickness, but sickness of heart, of emotions, of mind, of spirit. He's claiming as much territory as he can claim. And he's doing it with one goal: to steal everything that is worth something in our lives, to destroy us utterly, and to kill us forever. The devil hates you and has an evil plan for your life!

Unless you resist, rising up to declare that you will be a warrior in God's army, the devil will run right over you. He'll move in on every area of your life where you don't apply the blood of Jesus. He'll ride every one of your idle words of doubt, despair or fear for all it's worth. He'll launch fiery darts at you that will strike you wherever your life isn't covered with the armor of God. He'll seek you out to demolish God's purpose in you at every opportunity he gets.

The devil is not passive. He's not a laid-back enemy. The Bible says he's constantly stalking like a roaring lion, seeking out whom he may destroy. He's on the prowl. And unless you do your part by developing a warrior's mentality, you're in line to be his next victim, the next casualty on the battlefield.

Let's enlist in God's army right now so we can learn how to fight. Then we can become the warriors God wants us to be.

Close the Door on the Devil Today

1) Get a picture in your mind of a big God and a little devil. The devil isn't omniscient, omnipresent or omnipotent. That means he doesn't know everything, he isn't everywhere and he can't do everything. But God does, is and can!

2) Get a picture in your mind of your sins being covered fully by the blood of Jesus. A blood-stained altar stands

between you and the devil, and the devil cannot cross over that eternal dividing line.

3) Get a picture in your mind of having a blood transfusion, exchanging all of your old "Adam blood" with Jesus' blood.

4) Write your name below as a lasting reminder of your new "title" in Christ Jesus.

_____

(Your name here)
Heir of God With Christ Jesus

5) Say aloud today as a confession of your faith: "Jesus has come in the flesh and Jesus is Lord!"

Let's pray and agree together that you'll never forget that the devil's power over you is limited and that you must cast out the devil: "In the name of Jesus, I agree with you that this word is sealed forever in my heart. I declare today that I have been purchased by the blood of Jesus, and therefore I am a full heir of God with Christ Jesus. I am a recipient of all the promises and provisions purchased on my behalf on the cross of Calvary. The devil is a defeated devil. Jesus is Lord of lords, and He is Lord of my life. Amen."

FOUR

Enlistment:
The Blood of Jesus

Why have a strong military? Why do we need soldiers and armies and missiles?

I heard these questions asked sincerely by a number of people during the last presidential election. Yet the answer is simple: because a war is going on.

This war may not be fought out in great battlefields today in an open way so that we can readily count the casualties. But it's being fought nonetheless. Terrorism is rampant at an all-time high around the world. The nations of the earth are armed; nearly every country in the world has military spending at the top of its expense budget. And at the root of it all is the cause of war burning with a hot fire: a difference of opinion about who should be in power and who should control the resources of the earth.

The struggle has never been more intense. The war may not be obvious on the surface, but it's blazing with a fierce heat underground.

The same is true for the spiritual battle being waged against God's people. We are at war. Our enemy continues to stalk, to roar, to do everything in his power to steal, kill and destroy.

Fear, doubt and discouragement abound. Many of God's

45

people are feeling helpless, hopeless and hapless. They've lost their feeling of security and their sense of purpose. They're paralyzed in their panic.

Others are grief-stricken over losses they've experienced in their health, their finances and their families. They're in mourning.

Still others lie wounded. They're so bound by their troubles that they're hemorrhaging to death spiritually without anyone to bind up their sorrows and carry them to safety in the arms of Jesus.

These are descriptions of a people in wartime. The wounds, the grief and the panic are just as real as if bombs were dropping and bullets were flying.

Meanwhile, their hearts' cry is for peace. That's the cry of people who know they're in war.

They yearn for freedom. That's the cry of people who are under seige. They long for freedom from bombardment, freedom to live their lives without the constant threat of destruction, the constant killing, the constant pillage of their land and homes, the constant assault upon their minds and strength, the battering of their wills with false propaganda.

They yearn to be free, to live in victory, to experience the peace that passes all understanding. So how do they get that peace and freedom?

The Bible says, "The truth will make you free" (John 8:32). Freedom lies in knowing the truth. And that doesn't mean just with your head. Knowing the truth means to experience it with your entire being—mind, emotions, will.

What is the truth? The question should really be *who* is the truth? The truth is Jesus Christ. (See John 14:6.)

How do we get that truth inside us? How do we experience that truth? How do we have the gospel or the good news of Jesus as our Savior and Lord? The key is the blood of Jesus.

46

The Blood of Jesus

We who have attended church services for any length of time know the old songs about the blood of Jesus:

What can wash away my sin?
　Nothing but the blood of Jesus.
What can make me whole again?
　Nothing but the blood of Jesus.
Oh, precious is the flow that makes me white
　　as snow;
　No other fount I know,
　Nothing but the blood of Jesus.

　　　　　　　　　　　　　—Robert Lowry

There is a fountain filled with blood,
　Drawn from Emmanuel's vein,
And sinners plunged beneath that flood,
　Lose all their guilty stains.

　　　　　　　　　　　　　—William Cowper

We sing of the blood cleansing us of sin; of making us whole—body, mind and spirit; of being the most precious thing we can experience in our lives. The blood of Jesus. Nothing can take its place. Nothing can do what it does. Nothing can have the impact it has.

Experiencing the reality of the blood of Jesus is not only our entrance into the army of God. It's also the means for our continual re-enlistment in God's army on a daily basis. It's the way to peace and freedom.

By "experiencing the reality" I don't mean just knowing about the blood of Jesus. Mere knowledge about the blood won't set you free from the snares of the enemy, any more than mere knowledge about guns will fire one if you're a soldier. Knowing about the blood of Jesus must be coupled with experiencing it at work in your life, flowing through your veins, giving you life's substance on a continual basis in every area of your being.

By now you may be saying, Why all this emphasis on the blood of Jesus? That's all just a symbol; it's not something I can experience. I don't see how it applies to my life.

I disagree. The blood of Jesus is a reality for us today. It's the key to getting into God's army and it's the key to being a warrior. To have the blood of Jesus flowing through your being means you're God's soldier in the world today.

What the Bible Says About the Blood of Jesus

We've already seen what the Bible says about the blood of Jesus: "And they overcame him [the accuser of the brethren, the devil, the thief, Satan] by the *blood of the Lamb* and by the word of their testimony, and they did not love their lives to the death" (Rev. 12:11, italics added). The blood is our key to overcoming the devil.

Let that truth sink deep into your spirit. Don't just read those words and glide over them. Let them sink in. *The blood is your key to overcoming the devil.* It will set you free.

You can know all about an aspirin. You can recite the commercials word for word and even sing the jingles. You can know from past experience what happened to your headache when you took one. But all that knowledge won't do a thing for the headache you're experiencing now if you don't take one and let it get down inside you to do its work.

The same is true for this Scripture quotation and the others we'll examine. Read them, one by one, and then read them again and again. Meditate on them. Look them up in your Bible and mark them. Think about them and pray them. Don't just pray about them—pray them into your life. Let them become a part of the way you think, what you think about, the way you live out your life.

In the next few pages we'll look at several great Scripture verses about the blood of Jesus. There are many more in the Bible, of course. I encourage you to look them all up, using your concordance. Let them become part of your life. But for now, follow closely as we focus on these specific verses.

In Genesis 3:15, the Lord says to the devil: "And I will put enmity [which means "strife"] between you and the woman, and between your seed and her Seed [which is the Lord Jesus]; He [meaning Jesus, the Seed] shall bruise your head, and you shall [have the authority to] bruise His heel."

Here at the very beginning of the Bible, in the third chapter of the first book, God laid out the plan. He said that the devil would be able to bruise the heel of Jesus but that Jesus would crush his head.

The prophet Isaiah put up his prophetic periscope 760 years before the coming of Christ and predicted by the anointing of the Holy Spirit just how Jesus was going to crush the head of the enemy. He said, "Surely He has borne our griefs, and carried our sorrows, yet we esteemed Him stricken, smitten of God, and afflicted. But He was wounded for our transgressions, He was bruised for our iniquities, the chastisement for our peace was upon Him, and by His stripes we are healed" (Is. 53:4-5).

Jesus came to crush the head of the enemy by His suffering on the cross and by shedding His blood. From the time of Genesis to the time of Isaiah, the blood of lambs had been shed time and again through the sacrificial system, along with the blood of bulls and goats. But when Jesus came, the blood of the Lamb slain from the foundations of the earth was shed. (See Rev. 13:8.) It was the sacrifice of sacrifices, the blood sacrifice to end all blood sacrifices.

The blood sacrifice of Jesus made possible our being healed, saved and delivered. It put us into a position of peace and freedom from guilt, sorrow and affliction. Our new life didn't come by teaching. It didn't come by preaching. It didn't happen by good deeds. It happened by the blood sacrifice of Jesus of Nazareth who in shedding His blood became the Christ and our Lord.

Paul wrote about the blood of Jesus in Romans 3:21-25: "But now the righteousness of God apart from the law is revealed, being witnessed by the Law and the prophets, even the righteousness of God, which is through faith in Jesus Christ to all and on all who believe. For there is no difference; for all have sinned and fall short of the glory of God, being justified freely by His grace through the redemption that is in Christ Jesus, whom God set forth to be a propitiation by His blood." Note especially those last five words, *a propitiation by His blood.*

The passage in Romans continues: "through faith, to demonstrate His righteousness, because in His forbearance God has passed over the sins that were previously committed, to demonstrate at the present time His righteousness, that He might be just and the justifier of him who has faith in Jesus" (Rom. 3:25-26).

The blood is the way we are justified before God. It's the way our sins are removed so that we can stand before God in righteousness. In other words, we *cannot* stand before God unless we experience the blood sacrifice of Jesus. It's the key to entering the kingdom of God. It's the authority by which we enter heaven literally someday and spiritually right now.

The writer to the Hebrews said it another way: "Inasmuch then as the children [that is, we] have partaken of flesh and blood, He Himself likewise shared in the same, that through death He might destroy him who had the power of death, that is, the devil, and release those who through fear of death were all their lifetime subject to bondage" (Heb. 2:14-15).

What does that say to you and to me? It says that through the blood of Jesus, Satan's power has been destroyed. Say it aloud to yourself: "Through the blood of Jesus, Satan's power over any part of my life has been destroyed."

First John 3:8 tells us: "He who sins is of the devil, for the devil has sinned from the beginning. For this purpose the Son of God was manifested, that He might destroy the works of the devil." What are his works? To steal, kill and destroy. What is the antidote for those works? The blood of Jesus.

Look at Hebrews 9, starting with verse 12: "Not with the blood of goats and calves, but with His own blood He entered the Most Holy Place once for all, having obtained eternal redemption. For if the blood of bulls and goats and the ashes of a heifer, sprinkling the unclean, sanctifies for the purifying of the flesh, how much more shall the blood of Christ, who through the eternal Spirit offered Himself without spot to God, *purge your conscience from dead works to serve the living God?*" (italics added).

What does that mean to you and me? It means that we're free from mourning over the laws we've broken and free from the rituals that are only a form instead of life-giving food for our souls. Say it aloud to yourself: "The blood of Jesus purges my conscious mind from dead works to serve the living God."

Continuing on in Hebrews 9:15: "For this reason He is the mediator of the new covenant, by means of death, for the redemption of the transgressions under the first covenant, that those who are called may receive the promise of the eternal inheritance. For where there is a testament [a will] there must also of necessity be the death of the testator. For a testament is in force after men are dead." In other words, a will is only enforced after someone dies.

Do you understand what this is saying to you and me today? It's saying that the death of Jesus was necessary before we could fully receive all of the promises and rewards of the new covenant. We could never have experienced anything that we know of the saving, healing and delivering power of Jesus Christ without the death of Jesus and the shedding of His blood.

Blood sacrifice was necessary in the old covenant, too. Hebrews 9:19 tells about it: "For when Moses had spoken every precept to all the people according to the law, he took the blood of calves and goats, with water, scarlet wool, and hyssop, and sprinkled both the book itself and all the people, saying, 'This is the blood of the covenant which God has commanded you.' Then likewise he sprinkled with blood both the tabernacle, and all the vessels of the ministry. And according to the law almost all things were purged with the blood, and without the shedding of blood there is no remission [of sins].''

Read that last phrase one more time: *Without the shedding of blood there is no remission of sins.*

Some years ago America's seminaries and many so-called experts in theology took a turn away from the blood of Jesus. They stopped talking about it. They stopped preaching about it. Satan and his demons were laughing while liberal theologians made mockery of those who preached on the blood. They coined the phrase "butcher shop religion" to make fun of the blood of Jesus.

Nevertheless, I'm standing tall today—before the liberal theologians, before the devil, and before all the demons of hell—to declare to you the Word of God that "apart from the shedding of blood there is no remission of sins.''

Why are we focusing on all these Scripture verses? Because I've discovered in my teaching and preaching across this nation that many people, including many people who have been Christians for years and years, have never read these verses, have never memorized them, have never studied them, and do not have them locked into their spirits. Yet the blood of Jesus is the key to knowing Jesus Christ in a way that sets you free from the devil's power. "They overcame him by the blood of the Lamb." The shed blood of Jesus is the key to it all.

Look at just a few more verses. Hebrews 10:19 says: "Therefore, brethren, having boldness to enter the Holiest by the blood of Jesus...." The blood of Jesus is the way we enter the holiest level of life, the experience of life that is totally whole, totally healed, totally saved, totally delivered.

Hebrews 13:20-21 then gives the great apostolic benediction to this wonderful book that is filled with so many references to the blood of Jesus: "Now may the God of peace who brought up our Lord Jesus from the dead, that great Shepherd of the sheep, through the blood of the everlasting covenant make you complete."

The blood of Jesus makes us *complete* or whole. This word also means "full maturity." The blood of Jesus is the way we become complete and grow up to full maturity in our spiritual lives. Say it aloud to yourself: "The blood of Jesus is the way I enter into the holiest level of life, and it's the way I become complete and whole."

Turn to 1 Peter 1:18 and mark it in your Bible: "Knowing that you were not redeemed with corruptible things, like silver or gold, from your aimless conduct received by tradition from your fathers, but with the precious blood of Christ, as of a lamb without blemish and without spot."

"Precious." Of highest value. Worth something. The entire book of 1 Peter is marked by that word "precious": precious trials, precious faith, precious blood. These things are of high value and worth something to you and me today.

Finally, look at 1 John 1:7: "But if we walk in the light as He is in the light, we have fellowship with one another, and the blood of Jesus Christ His Son cleanses us from all sin." The verb tense here for "cleanses" means "continually cleansing." Day in and day out. It happens as we walk in the light of God's Word and continue in loving fellowship with other Christians.

The blood of Jesus continues to cleanse our lives. It didn't just happen on the cross nearly two thousand years ago. It didn't just happen on the day we accepted Jesus Christ into our lives as our personal Savior and Lord. It happens today, right now, and tomorrow and the next day. It's the blood of Jesus that continues to keep us clean from the sin, sickness, sorrow and destruction of this world.

Four Great Truths About the Blood of Jesus

All these passages, from Genesis to Revelation, are the foundation for four great truths about the blood of Jesus working in your life today:

1. Your sins and your sin nature are forgiven through the blood of Jesus.

Are you aware that you do more than commit sins—that you have a sin nature from the time you are born in your physical body to the time you are born anew by the Spirit of God? Are you aware that you were born into Adam's race under the reality of that sin nature?

We never teach our children to sin. They just begin to sin. You never taught your son or daughter to tell a lie, did you? You didn't sit down with them one day and say, "Son, I'm going to teach you to tell a fib." You didn't say to your daughter one day, "Daughter, I'm going to teach you how to tell a good lie." No, they were born with a sin nature that gave them that ability without any tutoring or prompting from you.

My mother and father didn't teach my sister, Libby, to hit me over the head with a can of hairspray one day when we were both children—and to hit me with such force that I went rolling down the stairs backward. They didn't have a class in my home to teach her how to wield that can of hairspray!

The fact is that we are all born in a condition of sin. And the blood of Jesus Christ is the only thing that can undo in our lives what the first man, Adam, did in his rebellious state against God. We are born with the need for a total blood transfusion. We need to trade in the Adam blood we got at our birth for the Jesus blood that was shed on the cross.

People often say to me, "Why do I need to be born again?" You need to be born another time because you were born wrong the first time. You were born with the wrong bloodline. Now you need to be born right.

Jesus is the only person ever born that didn't need to be born again. Why? Because He was born right the first time. He was conceived by the Holy Spirit, born of a virgin into this world without sin, and lived out His life without sin. He had the right bloodline from the very beginning, from the first cell of His being and from the first breath He took, right up through the very end of His earthly life.

When Jesus, the only sinless man who ever lived, went to the cross, He went there to become the sacrifice for our sin nature, as well as for all of the acts of sin that we have committed. When you look at Jesus with your spiritual eyes as He's hanging on that cross for you, in order to be truly born again in your spirit, you must say with every fiber of your being, "I want Your blood flowing through my life, cleansing out all of my old genetic pattern, my old sins, my old diseases, my old nature. I want a total blood transfusion. I want to have Your blood flowing through my arteries and veins. I want my heart to be as Your heart, pumping with Your life's blood. I want truly to become a child of God, with the right bloodline."

It's not just a theory or a nice idea. It's not just a symbol. It's reality. And it's the greatest reality that ever existed or ever could exist: to know the blood of Jesus in your life as an experience you have not just once but every day.

The blood of Jesus turns you from a sinner into a child of God. It turns you from living the life of "the old man" into a "new creation" (2 Cor. 5:17). It gives you the spiritual genetic code to become a warrior of God, with power to defeat the enemy and to enter into peace and freedom.

2. The blood of Jesus has broken Satan's legal hold on your life.

Satan no longer has any legal right to you once you have had a total transfusion of Jesus' blood into your life. Of course, the enemy of your soul will lie to you about that, which really isn't surprising since telling a lie is all that the enemy knows how to do. He will tell you that he has a right to your life, to your mind, to your business, to your spirit, to your physical body, to your entire person. He'll tell you that he has a right to your family and your job and your church. But the truth is that the enemy has no legal right over you or over anything that pertains to your life once you have had a total transfusion of Jesus' blood.

That doesn't mean we won't face struggles. All of us have had different troubles in our lives and we have struggled in our hearts over different things. But the devil lies when he comes and says to you, "That's just the way it's going to be. That's just the way it is in your life." He tries to convince you that the struggle you face is a permanent condition of your life rather than a battle you're in.

For a long period in my life I struggled with doubt. Spirits of doubt plagued me, causing me to doubt that I was truly saved and that I truly belonged to God. Have you ever doubted that way? Perhaps not, but I've discovered many, many people who have doubted their salvation or their deliverance from an evil situation or circumstance.

The enemy would come and attack my mind by saying, "If you were saved, you wouldn't have thought that thought," or "If you were truly delivered from sin, you wouldn't have done that."

One day I had had enough of that harassment. I resisted the enemy by saying, "Spirit of doubt, I resist you steadfastly by the blood of Jesus. I belong to One who bought me by His own blood. I belong to Jesus. Therefore, I do not belong to doubt and in the name of Jesus, doubt, you must go out of my life!"

You may be saying, But can I really say that? Yes, you can.

I paid fifty dollars for the Bible that's sitting here on my desk as I'm writing these words. If the man from the bookstore came in and said to me right now, "Larry, I'm taking back this Bible; it's mine," I would turn to him and say, "No, you aren't. I have a receipt. You put a price on that Bible. I paid it. Therefore, this Bible is not yours; it's mine." And I would have the full authority of the law to back me up.

The same is true for your life as it stands before God. Once you have traded in your Adam blood for Jesus' blood by an act of your will and your faith, then the ownership of your life has been transferred. Jesus has paid the price for your eternal soul; Satan no longer has any claim to you. Jesus was wounded for your transgressions and bruised for your iniquities. The chastisement of your peace was put upon Him and by His stripes you are healed (see Is. 53:5). He paid the price in full.

You've been released from the power of death, from fear and from all kinds of problems that Satan might try to put in your life. He broke the devil's hold on your life and released you from it. Say it aloud: "Jesus destroyed the devil by His blood and released me."

A man came to me several years ago and in the course of our counseling session said, "Pastor Larry, I'm a homosexual."

I said, "You are?"

He said, "Yes, I am."

"Who told you that?"

"What do you mean?"

"Who told you that you are a homosexual?"

"Well," he said, "I've never thought about who told me that. I just thought that was my orientation to life."

I said, "Well, my Bible says in the beginning God created the heavens and earth, and then He created man and woman. He created Adam. Then the Bible says He created Eve. And He put the two together. The Bible doesn't say God created Adam and Bruce."

Then I spoke to this man in compassion and love, because none of us—from the position as an heir of Adam—is immune to getting all mixed up about who we are. People are mixed up in their thinking about all kinds of issues of life, from the way they're overspending their credit cards to their lusting in the flesh and having a one-night fling. The world and the devil say to them, "You were made that way." In the lineage of Adam, we're all confused.

But my Bible says that once we're in the lineage of Christ, we're new creations. The Bible gives us a new picture of who we are and how we are to live.

I said to this young man, "Now in Adam the devil really could tell you anything about yourself and the argument might be very convincing, or even true. He could tell you that you could be Superman if you would only risk flying off a building, and people are buying that line all the time. But that doesn't mean that the devil is telling you the truth about yourself. In fact, if the devil is talking to you about yourself, you can be 100 percent certain that he's telling you the very opposite of the truth. He's a liar and always has been and always will be. He's not capable of telling the truth."

He looked at me as if the light was starting to dawn.

"But in Jesus Christ," I continued, "you are not a homosexual. That may have been your orientation in your state of having Adam blood. But that's not your state in Jesus Christ."

"Why do you say that?" he asked.

"Because of the blood of Jesus. Once you have a total transfusion of Jesus' blood, you are a new creation. You are a son of the most high. You have royal blood and homosexuality is not a part of your bloodline."

"What do I have to do?" he asked.

I said, "Repent of the sin in your life, ask God to forgive you according to your acceptance of the blood sacrifice of Jesus on the cross, quit thinking and believing that you are a homosexual, and start claiming in the name of Jesus that you are a new creation in Christ."

I led that young man in a prayer, commanding that spirit of lying and that spirit of homosexuality to stop harassing him. We agreed together in the name of Jesus that he was a new creation in Christ.

In the days to come he had to work hard to stand firm in his faith about who he was in Jesus. But that counseling session was the beginning of a new life for my young friend. Fourteen years have passed since that afternoon we prayed together, and today he is married and has a beautiful child. They are members of my church. Hallelujah! That's something to shout about.

What legal hold is the devil trying to keep on your life? Is he lying to you about the strength of your body, telling you that you will always be sick or prone to a certain disease or ailment? Is he lying to you about your financial condition, telling you that you will always struggle to pay your bills each month?

Rise up and resist that lie. Say, "Devil, you liar! You have no legal hold on my life. By my faith in the blood of Jesus, I no longer need to have anything to do with you. I have been bought by the risen Savior and Lord, Jesus Christ. So get out of my life, and get out now!"

You can do it. You have the right to do it once you have accepted the blood of Jesus in your life and have experienced its delivering power.

3. We receive the presence of the Lord through the blood of Jesus.

I'm not talking about the time when you were first saved or born again. I'm talking about a daily experience of the presence of Jesus. Everyone I've ever talked to wants to experience the presence of God and needs it in their lives.

How do we come to know the presence of God? Hebrews 10:19 says, "Having therefore, brethren, boldness to enter the presence of God, to come in to the Holiest of all by the blood of Jesus."

Most people I know try to come to God just about any way other than by the blood of Jesus. They may not even realize what they're doing. But they're coming to God with this kind of attitude:

"God, I haven't cursed anybody this week. God, I haven't been mean to my wife this week. God, I haven't been too lustful this week. God, I gave my tithe—at least I think I did, I'm not sure, but if I didn't I'll make it up to you next week. God, I've been trying real hard all this week to be a good person and a good Christian. So, God, please give me something so I can feel Your presence."

Do you know what that kind of talk is? It's the talk of a person who's trying to enter God's presence on the basis of his or her own good works. Yet in ourselves, no matter what we do or what we attempt, we can never be good enough for that.

The Bible says you enter His presence not by your righteousness but according to the righteousness of Jesus Christ. And He procured that righteousness for you on the cross by shedding His blood. His shed blood is your ticket—and your only ticket—into the presence of God.

How grieved God must be as He stands in the portals of heaven with bucketsful of glory, tons of anointing and showers of blessing, only to have His beloved children standing outside in guilt and condemnation, self-doubt and unbelief, wringing their hands and saying, "How can I get good enough to get God to bless me?" The fact is, you'll never be good enough in your own right.

But the second great fact is that there was One who was good enough in His own right. He shed His blood on your behalf and He's alive today at the right hand of the Father, saying, "By My blood, you now have a key to the front door. Come on in!"

Experiencing this truth on a daily basis is vital. It's the only way I know to keep the reality of your forgiveness fresh. It's a constant reminder in your life that you cannot come to God on your own goodness but that you can come to Him by the shed blood of Jesus. And that keeps ever before you the reality of your deliverance—your deliverance not only from past sins, but from present troubles as well.

About ten years ago, I came to God and said, "O God, how do I pray? How does any person really pray?" As I prayed that prayer, I had a vision of the blood of Jesus in a basin on an altar. Also on the altar was a pile of my sins. Then in the vision I saw Jesus empty that basin of His blood and pour it over the altar of my life, covering everything that was on it.

In that moment, the blood of Jesus became real to me. In my spirit I cried out, "Oh, thank You, Lord, for what the blood has bought for me!" I was ushered into the presence of God in a way I had never known up until that moment. But since that day, I've gone into the presence of God day by day, week by week, and now year by year on that very basis—recalling and experiencing the blood of Jesus covering all of my life.

When I was in seminary I stood before my preaching class one day to give a sermon. I said, "Ah, the blood of Jesus!" as a part of my presentation. When I received the professor's evaluation, I discovered that he had given me a lower grade than I was expecting. In the margin he had written, "Too emotional." I wrote back, "Can't help it!" and turned the paper back in to him.

Once you've experienced the shed blood of Jesus covering your sins and your life, you'll never be able to speak casually about the blood of Jesus again. You'll never be lukewarm on the subject, because you'll be experiencing His presence on a day-by-day basis because of that blood.

4. You are made complete through the blood of Jesus.

That's the promise of the Lord Jesus Christ, who said in Hebrews 13:21, "I'll make you complete." If you experience the three realities we've already discussed—if your sins and your sin nature have been forgiven, if Satan no longer has any legal hold on your life, and if you know the presence of God through the blood of Jesus—then you'll experience this fourth reality automatically. You will grow up and mature and become complete. Your entire being will be made whole.

The man on the inside who started out as a weak little infant in Christ will begin to stand up, walk and manifest righteousness, peace and joy, even in the midst of crises. He will stand and say, "I shall not be moved," when he's facing the fiery darts of the enemy. The man on the inside will manifest the fruits of purity and holiness. He'll exert authority over the devil. He'll put his foot down and say to the enemy, "Not any more you don't!"

I've recently become aware that nearly every Saturday I seem to have an attack of some kind from the devil. Bad news or a crisis of some type will hit, or some kind of prank will be played. Not too long ago we awoke on a Saturday morning to find that somebody had put a chain and padlock on the gate in front of our house so that we couldn't leave. Now that's a little thing, but it kept me and my family from several appointments while we arranged to have the chain cut so we could leave our yard. It was a first-class annoyance—until I realized what was really happening, and I just laughed. The devil was trying to throw me off balance so I'd break the spiritual momentum I had going into the Sunday services. So I said, "Devil, if that's the best you can do to try to trip me up, you've read this ol' boy wrong."

The devil apparently still needs to learn that I won't take it from him, and that the more he hits me, the meaner I'll get. The harder I'll preach. The more I'll pray. The stronger I'll get.

The more I'm hit, the more I'll fight back. And that means my spiritual muscles will grow stronger and stronger. Why? Because the blood of Jesus is flowing through my veins. I'm being made complete through Christ Jesus.

Through the blood of Jesus, then, I have forgiveness. I have deliverance from the devil's power. I experience the daily presence of God. And I am being made complete and mature in my whole person. What transforming power!

Today the blood of Jesus will transform you from being a nice, sweet little Sunday Christian—someone who just dresses up and goes to church once a week to listen to a nice, sweet little sermon and sing a few songs—into someone who's an awesome spiritual fighting machine for God. It's the blood of Jesus that will transform you from a wimp into a warrior.

Have you ever seen a young man go off to the military? You may have even had that experience yourself. The young recruits are usually a little nervous, a little unsure. Even if they're acting self-assured and a bit cocky, most of them aren't feeling very confident deep down inside.

But then look at them when they come home after boot camp. They have their hair cut and their uniforms on. Their heads are held high and they walk in confidence.

What's made the difference? They now have inside information about what it means to be "in the military." They've been through the most rigorous training they've ever experienced, both physically and mentally. They've been shaped up into soldiers and given a soldier's mentality before they're to be shipped out to specific assignments. They'll look you right in the eye and say, "I am a soldier. I am a military man." And you know by the way they say it that they mean it.

I've seen that same transformation take place in people once they truly experience the blood of Jesus. They may have been a little insecure in their faith, a little unsure about what they should do and say as Christians. They may have lacked confidence about what their rights are within the spiritual realm.

But once they truly know in an experiential way the power of the blood of Jesus working in them, they are transformed from the inside out. By the blood of Jesus they are forgiven, delivered and given entrance into the presence of God daily. It causes them to mature and become complete in Christ Jesus.

They have become God's warriors. They will look you right in the eye and say without blinking, "I am the righteousness of God." And I know of no more powerful declaration that people can make about themselves.

You Are God's Righteousness!

At this point I can just hear some of you gasping, "The righteousness of God? Oh no, not me!" But listen very carefully to this point. I didn't say, "You are righteous." I said, "You are the righteousness of God." There's a big difference.

If your life has been covered by the blood of Jesus; if you've experienced the forgiveness of God through the blood of Jesus; if Satan has no legal hold over your life; if you're experiencing the presence of God through the blood of Jesus; if you're growing spiritually into a mature, complete, "perfected" person, then you're righteous from God's standpoint. It has nothing to do with you in your flesh. Your life has been covered completely by the blood, and God can no longer see your flesh or your sin. He only sees Jesus' shed blood covering you. Because Jesus is 100 percent righteous, you are righteous through the blood of Jesus.

Romans 5:17-19 says, "For if by one man's offense death reigned through the one, much more those who receive abundance of grace and of the *gift of righteousness* will reign in life through the One, Jesus Christ. Therefore, through one man's offense, judgment came to all men resulting in condemnation, even so through one Man's righteous act the free gift came to all men resulting in justification of life. For as by one man's disobedience many were made sinners, so by one Man's obedience many will be made righteous" (italics added).

When Adam sinned, sin, death and unrighteousness

began to reign. When Christ died to redeem us from sin, then eternal life and righteousness began to take hold.

Note that special phrase "gift of righteousness." Many people say, "I thought righteousness was something I had to obtain; I thought it was a state of being I had to work hard to get to."

But this passage says righteousness is a *gift*. It has nothing to do with works. And how is this gift given? By the shed blood of Jesus Christ.

You can't become righteous by trying harder. You can't perform well enough to be considered righteous. You can only receive it as a gift of God.

Romans 3:20-26 spells it out: "Therefore by the deeds of the law no flesh will be justified in His sight, for by the law is the knowledge of sin. But now the righteousness of God apart from the law is revealed, being witnessed by the Law and the Prophets, even the righteousness of God which is through faith in Jesus Christ to all and on all who believe. For there is no difference, for all have sinned, and fall short of the glory of God, being justified freely by His grace through the redemption that is in Christ Jesus, whom God set forth to be a propitiation by His blood, through faith, to demonstrate His righteousness, because in His forbearance God had passed over the sins that were previously committed, to demonstrate at the present time His righteousness, that He might be just and the justifier of the one who has faith in Jesus."

The "deeds of the law" can't justify you or put you into a position of righteousness. The law has one purpose: to show you that you're a sinner, to make you fully aware that you have sinned and come short of the glory of God. It's only through faith in the blood of Jesus that you're put into a position of righteousness.

Notice the last phrase of that passage, "the justifier of him which believeth in Jesus." This means that Jesus declares the one who believes to be righteous. The blood of

Jesus is our righteousness before God—not our attempts to be a good person.

Through all of my years growing up I was told, "Be good. Don't do bad things." And the more I tried, the more I realized that I couldn't "be good." The more I tried, the more I realized that I was going to do bad things anyway. The harder I tried, the behinder I got. I wanted to be good, but the law of sin was working in my Adam flesh. No matter how much I wanted to be good, I couldn't be.

But then I came to the foot of the cross and realized that Jesus became my sin—that He literally became sin for me. He became Abraham's ram caught in the thicket; Moses' paschal lamb at the exodus; the Old Testament sacrificial bulls and goats; the One of whom John the Baptist said, "Behold, the Lamb of God that takes away the sins of the world." And He became all those things for me.

Knowing that, I had to face squarely the fact that He became my righteousness. He's the only righteousness I have. And so the only righteousness I have is a gift. *Righteousness is a gift.* We must get that reality deeply engrained inside us.

The words "propitiation" or "expiation" refer to "a release effected by payment of a ransom." Only one person could pay that price—the spotless Son of God Himself. With that price, Jesus bought my righteousness.

I can stand boldly today before you and declare, "I am righteous," not because of anything I have done but because I am the righteousness of God in Christ. If you're ever to become an overcomer, a true warrior in God's army, you too must develop what I would call a "righteousness conscience."

Can you imagine saying to a young soldier, "Hi, soldier," and having him answer, "Oh, no, not me"? A young man who's been through boot camp has learned how to salute and say, "Yes sir, I am a soldier!"

That's true for God's people as well. You need to have

a "righteousness conscience" instead of a "sin conscience." The Bible says that the Holy Spirit came to convict the world of sin, righteousness and judgment (see Jude 15). Now everybody has a rather clear understanding of what it means to be convicted of their sins. Just about everybody I encounter knows they are a sinner. They know they sin and need forgiveness of their sins.

I've met very few people, however, who are convicted of their righteousness. Instead they think of themselves as a sinner. But if you've experienced the blood of Jesus, being a sinner no longer defines your life. You are the righteousness of God.

Second Corinthians 5:17 says, "If anyone be in Christ, he is a new creation." No longer do you need to try performing well enough to gain acceptance from God and others. No, you have become a new creature, a completely new species in God's eyes, and you are the righteousness of God.

If you're trying to perform your way into righteousness today, I say this to you: "You're not righteous. But He is." Jesus Christ took your sin, your unrighteousness and your would-be righteousness as filthy rags onto His own person, and He died your death.

The greatest news I ever heard in my life was the news that I no longer needed to struggle to measure up to someone else's standards. All I needed to do was to recognize that Jesus Christ was going to do my measuring up for me. Only then could I begin to understand and walk in the knowledge of Philippians 4:13: "I can do all things through Christ who strengthens me."

Once you take on the identity of being the righteousness of God, you have an answer every time the devil comes to you with some kind of condemnation about your weaknesses and faults. You can look him squarely in the eye and say, "Just look at the blood, devil. Just look at the blood of Jesus covering my life. That's my righteousness. That's my true identity. And nothing else matters!"

You might also memorize Romans 8:1 to quote to the devil: "There is therefore now no condemnation to those who are in Christ Jesus, who do not walk according to the flesh, but according to the Spirit." No condemnation! If you're in Christ, then you're walking after the Spirit.

Read on in Romans: "For the law of the Spirit of life in Christ Jesus has made me free from the law of sin and death. For what the law could not do in that it was weak through the flesh, God did by sending His own Son in the likeness of sinful flesh, on account of sin: condemned sin in the flesh, that the righteous requirement of the law might be fulfilled in us who do not walk according to the flesh, but according to the Spirit" (Rom. 8:2-3).

Jesus came to condemn sin in our flesh. And all we have to say is yes to the new creation He has caused us to be.

When Satan comes to me with condemnation, I say, "Oh, yes, I did all those things—and some you haven't even mentioned yet, Satan. But I have a righteousness conscience now, and my righteousness is not in my measuring up any more. My righteousness is in Jesus. It's a gift from Him."

When the devil comes and says, "You're never going to get it right. You're never going to succeed. You're never going to make it," then I come right back and say, "That's right. By myself I never can and never will. But there is One who did and who can and He's living in Me. He who is in me is greater than he who is out there in the world." (See 1 John 4:4.)

Revelation 12:11 says, "And they overcame him...." Who is "him"? The preceding verse calls him the "accuser of the brethren." That's precisely what the enemy comes to do: to accuse you of sin, of shortcomings, of faults, of not measuring up, of all your flaws and mistakes. The enemy comes to say, "You'll never make it because you're such a louse."

But Revelation 12:11 says, "And they overcame him...."

They *overcame* him. And they did it how? "By the blood of the Lamb and the word of their testimony."

If Satan comes to you with a club of condemnation to beat you up with his accusations, and you give in to him, then you've lost right at that point. But if you say, "I'm more than a conqueror through Him who loves me and gave Himself for me," then you have the weapons of the blood of the Lamb and the word of your testimony. You become the overcomer.

Colossians 2:15 says that Jesus made "an open show" of the principalities and powers, and He triumphed over them. That is the same Jesus you have living in you. Have you traded in your Adam heart for the heart of Jesus? Have you traded in your Adam blood for the blood of Jesus? Have you been forgiven of your sins and your sin nature by the blood of Jesus? Then you've passed from the place where Satan had a legal hold on your life to the place where you can experience the presence of God and grow into completeness, wholeness and maturity because of the blood of Jesus.

Have you traded in your mind-set of being clothed in the filthy rags of your sin for the mind-set of being clothed in the garments of righteousness—not a righteousness of your own works but the righteousness that is the gift of God to you through the shed blood of Jesus? Then you're in God's army. You're His warrior. You're His battle-ax to tear down principalities, powers and strongholds of the enemy.

Go look in your mirror and say, "I am the righteousness of God through Christ Jesus!" Then come right back so we can talk about our first priority as warriors.

Close the Door on the Devil Today

1) Repeat aloud to yourself these phrases and mean them: Today, through the blood of Jesus, Satan's power over any part of my life has been destroyed, including that area

I've always wondered about.

Today the blood of Jesus purges my conscious mind from dead works to serve the living God. I will no longer live in my works or trust them for my reputation before God.

Today the blood of Jesus is the way I enter into the holiest level of life, and it's the way I become whole and complete. I am becoming whole and complete.

2) Get a picture in your mind of your sins heaped in a pile on a beach. Then suddenly a great wave comes and washes them away, leaving the beach completely free of debris. In the same way, your sins are completely forgiven, and forgotten, when you become a new creation in Christ Jesus.

3) Get a picture of yourself tied up with ropes. Suddenly the ropes snap and you're free. In the same way, the blood of Jesus completely breaks all legal hold that Satan has had on your life.

4) Write your name in the space below as a lasting declaration:

_____

(Your name here)
Free and Becoming Complete in Christ Jesus!

Let's pray and agree together you'll never forget that the blood of Jesus is your salvation, your completion and your number-one weapon against the devil: "In the name of Jesus, I agree with you that this word is sealed forever in my heart. I declare today that I have forgiveness. I am delivered from the devil's power. I can and do experience the daily presence of God. I am being made complete and whole. I am the righteousness of God. The blood of Jesus is my gift from God, and it's my number-one weapon against the enemy. Amen."

FIVE

Reveille:
Beginning With Prayer

For more than a decade now, I've started every morning by spending an hour or more in prayer.

I'm not telling you that so you'll pat me on the back and say, "Oh, Larry, that's wonderful"—and then under your breath add, "for you, brother." I don't have any more pride in that statement than a soldier might have in saying, "Every day of my life begins with reveille at dawn."

I really don't feel I have any more choice in the matter than an obedient soldier does in fulfilling his duties in the military. He's in the army so his day begins with reveille. I've enlisted in the army of God's spiritual warriors, so my day begins with my "spiritual reveille."

I don't choose to do this because I'm naturally a "morning person." I find it just as difficult as the next guy to roll out of bed on a dark, blustery winter's morning, turn off the alarm, put my feet on the floor, get dressed and go down to the church to pray.

I don't do this because one day I just decided I would be some kind of superspiritual person, and this would be the badge of my spirituality. In fact, it's my experience that most people who consider themselves to be superspiritual don't think they *need* to pray an hour a day.

No, I started praying an hour every morning because God called me to do it. He made it very clear to me that an hour of prayer each morning was a part of what it would take if I was ever going to become a spiritual warrior—a warrior capable of overcoming the devil in my life and tearing down principalities, powers and darkness on this earth.

The Spirit asked me a simple question: "Could you not tarry one hour?" That was the same question Jesus asked His apostles in the Garden of Gethsemane just hours before His crucifixion. It stuck in my mind and heart until it became the deepest desire of my life to please God and to begin each day in His presence.

I've learned a great deal about prayer—about the power of prayer, the purpose of prayer, the need for prayer—as the years have rolled by. But much of what I've learned is summed up in the word *first*.

The First Order

First. That's also a part of the meaning of "reveille" to a soldier. At reveille, trumpets or some other signal begin the day and summon a soldier to get about his duty. Reveille is the first order of the day for the soldier. It's the first order for God's soldiers, too.

Jesus said it in Matthew 6:33: "Seek *first* the kingdom of God, and His righteousness, and all these things shall be added to you." But what does it mean to seek first the kingdom of God?

I believe it means to make God and His kingdom your first priority. It means to establish your life pattern so that the kingdom is the first thing you're looking for—and that includes the first thing you seek every morning. If the kingdom of God is first, then seeking God and pursuing His righteousness are at the top of your agenda. Every success in the life of a spiritual warrior of God can be attributed to *seeking first* the kingdom of God and His righteousness.

72

The Bible says everything else falls into line when you and I make the kingdom of God and His righteousness our top priority, our first item on life's agenda. Everything you need—the health and strength to get through the day; the joy of good relationships with family, friends and co-workers; the money to pay your bills; the direction and wisdom to make the right decisions—comes when you make your "reveille" the seeking of God's kingdom and His righteousness.

So how do you spend an hour in prayer? That's a good question to ask.

I love that question how. I grew up attending a church where the pastor spent a great deal of time telling us *what* we should and shouldn't do. Yet time and time again, even as a boy and then as a teenager, I found myself asking, But how?

How does Christianity work? How can my needs be met? How can I experience God? How can I know with certainty that I'm saved and that I'll be with the Lord when I die? How can I become a spiritual warrior? If there's one question I come to again and again as I prepare sermons, write books and lead seminars, it's how.

How do we pray? That's the same question the apostles asked Jesus. In Matthew 6:9-13 we find Jesus' answer:

> In this manner, therefore, pray: Our Father in heaven, hallowed be Your name. Your kingdom come. Your will be done on earth as it is in heaven. Give us this day our daily bread. And forgive us our debts, as we forgive our debtors. And do not lead us into temptation, but deliver us from the evil one, for Yours is the kingdom and the power and the glory for ever. Amen.

Now if you're like me, it takes about twenty seconds, give or take a few, to say those words all the way through once. So how does the Lord's prayer become a spiritual reveille to us? In my experience, you can sum it up in three words: Set, ready, go.

You might think at first that I mean instead 'ready, set, go' like we used to say at the start of a race when we were children. But no—this time the order is set, ready, go. These three words are critical for establishing your spiritual reveille.

Think of these words in the context of football if that will help you remember the order. I talked to a Dallas Cowboy football player recently, so I have what I'm about to say on good authority.

When professional football players crouch down for those few seconds before a play begins, they're getting "set" physically. Then, during those one, two or three seconds that the numbers signifying the play are being called out by the quarterback, the rest of the players are getting "ready" mentally.

The numbers called out by the quarterback have meaning to the players, so the players rehearse them in their minds one last time. These are the "call numbers" for a particular play—a pattern of motion. Mentally, the team members are going over just where they are about to move in the next moment.

Finally, when the ball is snapped from the center to the quarterback, the players "go." And they'd better move quickly and with all their energy if they want the play to succeed.

Set, ready, go. That's the key to making the Lord's prayer your spiritual reveille. Here's how.

Get Set

When you come to the Lord in prayer, the first part of the prayer is your time for "getting set." You begin by praying, "Father in heaven, hallowed be Your name. Your kingdom come. Your will be done in earth as it is in heaven."

In this time you're setting your affection on the Lord, turning your attention to Him. You're focusing on His name, His kingdom and His will. You're getting things settled on the inside.

You're declaring that He is your everything. You're taking your eyes off yourself and setting your eyes on the One who has come to meet every need in your life. He's your righteousness. He's your provision. He's the source of your healing. He's your Lord, your Savior; your deliverer, your protector; your counselor, your comforter; your source of supply; the vine of which you're a branch; your friend.

In this time you "hallow" or remember and revere His name. You pray the name of God into your life. You pray the attributes associated with the name of Jesus into your being.

Lift up the name of Jesus in those first few minutes of your prayer time. Who is He to you? Recall what He's done for you, and give Him thanks for it!

"Our Father in heaven, hallowed be Your name." You're hallowing the name of the Father, the name of Jesus, as you offer thanksgiving and praise to Him.

Next we pray, "Your kingdom come. Your will be done." But what are the attributes of God's kingdom? And what is His will?

First of all, God's will is that you be saved and delivered from everything that will trip you up and keep you from doing the kingdom-building work God has set out for you to do.

God's will is also that you be filled with the Holy Spirit and that you experience His comfort and counsel today— not just once in the distant past, but right now, in the very circumstances of the hour.

God's will is that you be whole. Jesus spent much of His earthly ministry healing those who were sick, afflicted and tormented. He said often, "Be thou made whole." Wholeness is the key word for your healing: whole in body, in mind, in emotions, in your relationships with other people, in your finances, in your spirit.

God's will is that you prosper, that your efforts be fruitful and that you reap God's rewards. And God's will is that you defeat the devil and conquer your spiritual enemies.

Pray that God's will *will* be done in your life—today!

Then pray the attributes of the kingdom into reality in your life. Declare it to be so for you today, right where you are.

What are the attributes of the kingdom of God? The kingdom is where joy, peace and righteousness reign supreme. These realities are the very atmosphere of heaven, and your prayer is that this atmosphere will surround you here on the earth. Command it to be so. Declare it to be so.

Are you experiencing joy in your family? in your job? in your church? in your relationships with colleagues, friends and neighbors?

Are you experiencing peace in your family? in your job? in your church? in your relationships with colleagues, friends and neighbors?

If not, put your foot down and say with all your heart, "I'm settling this, no matter what comes my way. I will have the peace, joy and righteousness of the kingdom of God in my life. I will have the will of God done in my life. Everything related to the kingdom of God will be magnified, amplified, exemplified and glorified through my life today!"

When you pray, "Your kingdom come. Your will be done on earth as it is in heaven," you're setting your priorities for the day. Think back to that football player getting "set" on the line before the play begins. What happens if he doesn't get his cleats firmly planted in the turf? What happens if he's still standing straight up when the play begins? He gets run over!

The same thing will happen to you if you don't get set. Principalities and powers are at work in our world right now that have never been on the scene before. Satan has kept them in a dark hole of hell until this age, and he's loosed them at this last hour to pull down ministries, ruin believers and destroy your life. So get set.

Resolve within yourself that your affection, your eyes, your goals, your priorities, your desires, your thoughts, your actions and your words will be set on hallowing the Father's name, on seeing that His kingdom comes to the earth, on making sure His will is done.

Get Ready

"Give us this day our daily bread and forgive us our debts as we forgive our debtors." That's the way we get ready.

I ask God to provide my "daily bread." He says to ask, and so I do. I ask Him to give me what I need to feed and clothe my family, to provide a house for them, to educate my children, and whatever else they need. I pray for the things I need personally. I pray for the things we need in the church. I pray specifically.

When I pray, I remind myself and God of the seeds I and others have planted for that harvest of supply. For example, as I pray for my church, I say, "Lord, we have sown our seeds in faith, by giving to missions. We're providing the salaries for these missionaries and praying for their work and helping to pay the expenses for their mission stations and clinic. Those are seeds we have sown. We praise You for providing the seed in the first place and we praise You for giving us the opportunity to sow it. It's on that basis we come to You expecting harvest. We're expecting our daily bread so that the needs of our church can be met today. God, You know what it will take this week to operate this whole church. I commit it now into Your hands."

Now you can only pray that way if you have indeed planted your seeds in faith. For many, this prayer leads to conviction, a realization that you haven't planted seeds and need to. If that's the case for you, set yourself to planting.

But once you've planted your good seeds (of time, prayer, work, skills, money) in good soil, with faith believing, what a privilege it is to stand before the Lord, Jehovah-jireh—your provider—and pray, "Give us this day our daily bread!"

"Of course," you say, "you're a pastor, Larry, so you should pray that way for your church. I'm just a lay person."

You have a responsibility as a lay person to pray for your church just as much as the pastor who leads you. In fact, you have a responsibility to pray for your pastor. We're all to pray for those in authority over us, including spiritual authority. (See 1 Tim. 2:2.) You have a responsibility to pray as well for those in need within your church, and to pray one for another that you might be healed. (See James 5:16.)

But this prayer is not just for your church; it's for every area of your life. It's for your personal needs and the needs of your family. So make the request personal: Give *me* this day *my* daily bread.

What are you doing when you pray this way? You're getting ready to receive. You're putting your expectancy on the line. You're facing the day with joy because something good is about to happen to you. You're facing the day with peace because your needs will be met.

Next we pray: "Forgive us our debts as we forgive our debtors." Do you realize that as long as you have guilt or unforgiveness in your life, you can't be "ready" to walk out the events of your day in the victory of the Holy Spirit?

One thing can stop the flow of God's righteousness into your life—the righteousness that comes about through repentance, forgiveness and applying the blood of Jesus to your total life. Unforgiveness will stop it. You can't receive forgiveness from God if you don't forgive others. It's plainly stated time and time again in the Scriptures:

Be kind to one another, tenderhearted, *forgiving one another, just as God in Christ also forgave you* (Eph. 4:32, italics added).

Therefore, as the elect of God, holy and beloved, put on tender mercies, kindness, humbleness of mind, meekness, longsuffering; *bearing with one another, and forgiving one another, if anyone has a complaint against another; even as Christ forgave you, so you also must do* (Col. 3:12-13, italics added).

Be merciful, just as your Father also is merciful. Judge not, and you shall not be judged. Condemn not, and you shall not be condemned. *Forgive, and you will be forgiven* (Luke 6:36-37, italics added).

Jesus said to His disciples: "If a brother sins against you, rebuke him"—in other words, let him know he has trespassed, call it to his attention, let him know that you feel hurt by his actions—but "if he repents, forgive him" (Luke 17:3). Once your brother has acknowledged his wrong and repented of it, you must forgive him. And Jesus went on to say that even if your brother sins against you seven times in a day, and each time repents, you must forgive. There's no legitimate reason for holding back forgiveness when repentance is offered (see Luke 17:4).

Peter came to Jesus and said, "How many times shall I forgive any brother who sins against me? Seven times seven?" Jesus answered him, "*Seventy* times seven!" In other words, keep on forgiving. Don't let any speck of unforgiveness take root in you and grow into a bitterness that inhibits your continuing ability to forgive. (See Matt. 18:21-22.)

Unforgiveness takes many forms: judgmentalism, criticism, unresolved conflicts, unresolved arguments and feuds, slander, gossip, jealousy. But how often do we come before God and truly ask Him to forgive us for these things? How often do we ask others to forgive us for these things which we have done against them?

How many times do we seek to bind evil spirits and fail, because we hold unforgiveness in our hearts? Our coming against the devil is in vain until we can fight as forgiven men and women of God. And to be forgiven, we must first forgive.

Let's get honest in the church. Jesus doesn't want us to live like the Pharisees. They never wanted to face their own insecurities and blind spots. Instead they criticized others for the very faults they themselves possessed.

Guilt will bind you. It will tie you in knots spiritually. So get free. And the only way to do that is to confess your sin to the Lord, then choose to walk in forgiveness of others.

How many of us can stand and say, "I don't need forgiveness. I pray for justice on the judgment day"? Do you really want justice? I certainly don't. I want *mercy*.

Every one of us in our right mind recognizes that we've sinned and we do sin and we come short of the glory of God, so that it's only by His mercy that we aren't consumed. We're given that mercy when we show mercy to others. So let it sink deep down in your heart: You are forgiven as you forgive.

How do you pray this reality in a practical way? Ask God to reveal to you your sins and your trespasses against others. Then repent of those sins, and ask God to forgive you for them.

Release and forgive those who have hurt you or sinned against you. Turn them over to God, then choose to walk out your day in that attitude of forgiveness. Live out what Scripture says: "Bless those who curse you, and pray for those who spitefully use you." (See Luke 6:28.) Call out their names to the Lord. Release them to Jesus; ask God to forgive them and to have mercy on them.

How does this get us ready for our day? When we walk in forgiveness, we walk in paths of righteousness. We are experiencing the righteousness of the kingdom of God. Indeed we become the righteousness of God walking through this earth as living witnesses of His power, peace and joy.

We have joy because we know that Satan cannot penetrate or dominate whatever is the righteousness of God. He cannot cross the bloodline. If our trespasses have been covered by the blood of Jesus, Satan cannot cross over that line into our lives. That assurance gives us peace which passes all understanding.

When we stand in forgiveness, without guilt and without condemnation of others, then we have built a hedge around us that Satan cannot penetrate. Hear that again: Satan cannot penetrate or dominate a person who receives forgiveness, forgives others and walks in that forgiveness. What freedom that gives us!

"Give us this day our daily bread and forgive us our debts as we forgive our debtors." You're ready for the day when you can pray that out of your heart. You're ready to receive God's provision and abundance. You're ready to see how God will meet your daily needs. You're ready to face any person, because you have no enemies. You're no longer afraid of what any person can say or do against you. You're freed up inside to have joy, peace and righteousness in your life. And Satan is bound from crossing over into your life because you have given him no "guilt bridge" to use. You're ready for God's agenda to unfold in your life!

And Then Go!

"Lead us not into temptation, but deliver us from the evil one." This is the prayer of resistance. The Bible says we are to resist the devil so that he will flee from us. (See James 4:7.)

I guarantee you that the enemy will come after you. He

81

wants your life, your health, your mind, your money, your family, your mission in life. He's out to steal, kill and destroy whatever he can get his hands on. That's the down side.

But the up side is this: When you put on the whole armor of God and stand in resistance, he will—he *must*—flee from you. I've heard people say again and again, "You don't need to resist the devil. Just say, 'Lord, resist him for me.'" But that's not what the Bible says.

The Scripture says *you* must resist the devil, and he will flee from *you*. Jesus has already resisted the devil. The devil has already fled from Him. Now *you* are the one responsible for standing against the devil today.

How can you get prepared to resist the devil? By putting on the whole armor of God. So the entire next chapter is devoted to just that—how to put on the uniform of a warrior. It's up to you to
- gird *your* loins with truth;
- put on *your* breastplate of righteousness;
- don *your* helmet of salvation;
- wear *your* shoes of the preparation of the gospel of peace;
- take up *your* shield of faith; and
- pick up *your* sword of the Spirit.

Nobody else will do it for you. I'll help you learn how to do it, but it will be up to you to do it in your own life. As you put on those pieces of armor, you need to be praying all the time, "I will resist the devil steadfastly in the faith every time he comes against me today. I'm wearing the right kind of armor. I'm prepared to resist."

Meanwhile, you're also asking God, "Lead me not into temptation." I pray, "Lord, I believe You are the good Shepherd and You will lead me, Your sheep, into paths of righteousness today for Your name's sake. I'm trusting You to order my steps because You said that the steps of a righteous man are ordered by You."

Memorize that verse if you don't know it already: "The steps of a good man are ordered by the Lord, and He delights in his way" (Ps. 37:23). Notice that phrase, "He delights in his way." God's way will be joy-filled, peace-filled and a delight. It won't be a way filled with temptations and snares.

With this prayer, you're saying, "Lord, Your truth will dominate me today. Righteousness will be all over my heart. My feet will be ready to walk in the spirit today wherever You lead me. I'm putting up the shield of faith to quench every fiery dart of the devil. I'm pulling down my headgear so my mind will be only on Your salvation. Your word will be in my mouth today as the sword of the Spirit penetrating the shadows of darkness. I'm ready to go in You, God!"

Then you begin to move into praise: "For Yours is the kingdom and the power and the glory forever!" You complete your prayer time, your hour of reveille with the Lord, by praising and magnifying His greatness.

Do you know what you'll be doing for ten thousand times ten thousand times ten thousand years? You won't be wondering whether your house is paid for, or whether the pews in the church are the right color, or who gets the promotion at work, or what kind of car your wife is driving. Your concern will be God's glory, His power and His kingdom. You'll be worshipping, praising, magnifying Him.

What do your praises do? They allow God to release His angels to protect you. The Bible says that God inhabits the praises of His people. (See Ps. 22:3.) The angels are present, too, anytime praise is voiced, anytime someone cries, "Holy, holy, holy is the Lord!" The Bible says as well that God gives His angels charge over you (Ps. 91:11; Matt. 4:6). He sends them to be "ministering servants" on your behalf (Heb. 1:14).

Do you realize what happens when you sit back and choose not to go forth and praise God? The angels fold their wings; they're not active.

83

What happens if you walk up to John and said, "Boy, John, I've got some bad problems"? What does that do to John? He immediately feels bound in his spirit. He doesn't know what to do for you or to say to you because he immediately faces a wall of trouble that he perceives all around you.

But what happens if you say, "John, God's got it under control. God bless you, John. We're going to take this world for Jesus Christ. We really are!" How does that make John feel?

It blesses him. He has a point of agreement with you. He's heard an encouraging word to help him through his struggles. He's looking forward, and forward to a victory in God—not to the past or present where troubles abound.

When you voice praise to God, the angels become active all around you. They form a hedge of protection. They're not only present, but they're also at work to fight in the heavenly sphere for you. They're your ministering servants to hold back the powers of darkness so that you can walk in the paths of righteousness and experience the glory of God shining into your life.

Thank You, God, for the angels that protect us! Thank You, Lord, for the angels that have charge over us and that are activated by our praises!

When you walk out into your day in prayer, trusting God to lead you in righteousness and *not* into temptation; trusting God to deliver you from evil; believing with your whole heart and praising Him with your mouth that He *is* the kingdom, the power and the glory in your life and forever more; then you *go*. You move out into your daily life with the mind-set of resistance and the heartbeat of praise. You're focused on God, His kingdom and His will. You're set in Him and you've directed your heart and your footsteps toward Him.

You're ready to receive everything good that God has for you. You're free to walk in forgiveness, because you have freely forgiven. And you're looking for God's way—a path that's as far away from temptation and evil as you can get, and close to everything that is righteous.

You're prepared for a day of joy and peace. You're fully clothed with the armor of God. You're prepared for victory as you fight against the forces of darkness that come against you. You're fully awakened to perform your duties as God's warrior, and you're putting God first in your day, your priorities, your affections.

That kind of reveille in God gets you ready for revelry in the joy of the good things God has for you. It's a delight to walk with God in the victory of the Holy Spirit. It's pure happiness to know His will and to do it. It's unspeakable joy to experience the power of God flowing in your life and in the lives of your family, friends and associates. And that brings us to the final part of reveille.

Get Together

A soldier doesn't experience reveille alone. He gets together with the others from his barracks, his squadron, his troop unit. Reveille isn't an individual activity.

Neither is spiritual reveille when it operates in the most effective way. It's a good thing to spend an hour in the presence of the Lord to start your day. But it's a better thing if you get together with others from your family or your church.

You need to know—to experience fully—the fellowship of others in Christ. (See Heb. 10:25; 1 John 1:7.) You need to agree with others as you pray and take on the strongholds of the enemy. (See Matt. 18:19.) You need to be with others to pray for them and to have them pray for you. (See James 5:16.)

John Wesley, the father of the Methodist movement, said that the secret of that movement's power to change eighteenth-century England was twofold: *first*, early morning prayer meetings; and *second*, small home groups that met so the people might exhort and encourage one another in the Word.

I pray it will happen to us as it happened in the days of John Wesley's ministry. Morning prayer meetings and small groups are the basis for a revival that can sweep a land to bring salvation and deliverance to the lost and the suffering.

The military uses the word "muster" to refer to the calling of everyone together to take the roll. It's "all hands on deck" time.

Something else also happens when troops "muster." Usually that's when orders are given. Individual soldiers or groups of soldiers are given specific assignments.

The same thing happens when groups of believers get together under the leadership of the Holy Spirit. The Holy Spirit passes out assignments to God's people: "You two or three, get together and pray for that person to be delivered from the powers of evil." "You two go and help that person in their need." "You three or four get together and carry this sick one on his pallet to Jesus for healing."

That reception of divine instructions can't happen nearly as efficiently or as effectively if you're off in your corner having reveille in the Lord while another person is across town having reveille at a different hour.

It's time to get together. The body of Christ is a "we." It takes us all. And it takes us "mustered" as troops pulling together in the same army, as fellow warriors fully awake, fully set in our hearts, ready in our spiritual attitude, and encouraging one another and building up one another as we go into the world along paths of righteousness for His name's sake.

Wake up! It's time to get *set, ready and go together* for God.

Close the Door on the Devil Today

1) Set your alarm for an hour earlier than you normally rise in the morning. Open your Bible to Matthew 6:9. Place your alarm clock on top of your open Bible, and put both your alarm and your Bible across the room from your bed so you'll have to get out of bed to turn off your alarm. When you turn off the alarm, you'll see it sitting on your first priority for the new morning.

2) Begin looking today for a friend or friends with whom you can share this chapter. Ask them to consider prayerfully your meeting together for early morning prayer.

Let's pray and agree together you'll never forget that your reveille as God's warrior is prayer: "In the name of Jesus, I agree with you that this word is sealed forever in my heart. And, Lord, I declare that today is a new day for me in Your army. Help me to have the desire to pray. Help me to act on my faith and to do as You taught by Your words and Your example. Help me to start and never stop a morning reveille with You. Amen."

SIX

Putting on the Uniform:
The Whole Armor of God

S atan hates what I'm about to tell you in this chapter. It's a life or death matter—life to those who hear it, believe it and do it, and death to those who don't. But I'm trusting that the church triumphant will become the church militant so that life will flow, and life abundantly!

Remember again what Jesus said in Luke 12:31: "Do not fear, little flock, for it is your Father's good pleasure to give you the kingdom." Yet at the same time, in Matthew 11:12, we read that "from the days of John the Baptist until now the kingdom of heaven suffers violence, and the violent take it by force."

God wants to give us the kingdom. But there's only one way to receive what God wants to give, and that's by force—not force over men, not force over institutions, but all-out force over spiritual powers, principalities and rulers of darkness. Someone is trying to keep you from receiving the kingdom that God wants you to receive, and force is required to overcome that enemy.

Remember as well that we run this race of the gospel not just to go through the motions of running. We run to win! We run with a view toward winning the race and its prize. That's the Christian ethic.

People who think that we're on a stroll through the park don't understand the full message of the New Testament. The apostle Paul exhorted, "Run in such a way as to get the prize" (1 Cor. 9:24). He said, "I press toward the mark of the high calling of God, which is in Christ Jesus" (Phil. 3:14). Press on! Someone is trying to trip you up and take you on a detour to keep you from winning the race. So it will take concerted effort to win.

Something must rise up within you to say, "I won't let the devil take what belongs to the kingdom of God and what belongs to me and to my family *any more*. I won't just stand by and let him ravage our homes, take advantage of our children or gain any authority over our church."

The biggest lie Satan tells today is that "everything is OK." Everything is *not* OK. Most people I know need more deliverance, more health, more peace and joy in their hearts. And it will take effort, commitment, even force, to meet that need.

In Ephesians 6:10-18 we have a passage critical to our understanding of how to succeed as a warrior for God and win over the devil. Let's examine it step-by-step, beginning with verse 10: "Finally, my brethren, be strong in the Lord and in the power of His might."

When David was being chased by King Saul, the Scriptures say, "David's men gathered there at the cave of Adullam" (1 Sam. 22:1). These men were the outcasts of society, the dregs, the has-beens. The Bible says they were in "distress," "debt" and "discontent" (22:2). But as these men rallied around David and were led by him, they became known as "David's mighty men."

Many Christians today are feeling like the men who staggered out to Adullam's cave. But I promise you that if you'll rally around Jesus and stay close to the Holy Spirit, He'll cause you to become one of "God's mighty men" today. As Ephesians 6:10 says, you'll become "strong in the Lord and in the power of His might."

Why do we need to be strong in the Lord? Read on to verses 11-13: "Put on the whole armour of God, that you may be able to stand against the wiles of the devil. For we do not wrestle against flesh and blood, but against principalities, against powers, against the rulers of the darkness of this age, against spiritual hosts of wickedness in the heavenly places. Therefore take up the whole armor of God, that you may be able to withstand in the evil day, and having done all, to stand."

Verse 12 spells out clearly who the enemy is: principalities, powers, rulers of the darkness of this world and spiritual wickedness in high places. Sadly enough, many people today are being blinded by these very powers.

When we win over the devil, our spiritual eyesight gets sharper. On the other hand, if we get on a losing track with the enemy, our spiritual vision grows dim.

Verses 11 and 13 tell us the consequences of putting on the whole armor of God. These consequences are critical for our survival.

Eleven years ago I was on the staff of Beverly Hills Baptist Church when our pastor, Howard Conatser, had a heart attack. I was asked to assume the pastoral responsibilities of that church for six months on an interim basis. I was only twenty-two years old, just one year out of college, and I suddenly felt like the world had come down on my shoulders. I sensed a great need in my life. I was fighting from day to day against doubt and depression, feeling intense pressure to perform. I couldn't see how to walk in the victory that I knew God had promised me in His Word.

One day a Lutheran pastor came into my office. He was a member of our church at the time, no longer active in his denomination as a minister, and he spoke out of his pastor's heart: "Larry, do you put on the whole armor of God every day?"

Now I had taken three years of Greek when I was in Dallas Baptist College. In my third year of Greek, I took a class in which there were only three of us—the professor, one other student and myself. The object of our study together was the book of Ephesians. I studied every noun, every verb, every participial phrase that year. So I knew all about the book of Ephesians, including the sixth chapter.

With that study in mind, I leaned back in my chair and said to my friend, "Oh yes, I know all about putting on the whole armor of God. I even had a class in which we studied the sixth chapter of Ephesians in depth. I know about all the nouns and verbs and how it all fits together."

He said, "I didn't ask you if you knew *about* that passage. I'm asking whether you do what that passage says to do every day?"

I stared at him blankly, but he persisted. "Do you put on the whole armor of God every day?"

I scratched my spiritual head for just a second and realized once again that to know about the Word of God is one thing, but to do the Word of God is an altogether different thing. So I had to confess to him, "No, I don't do it."

"Well," he said, "let me show you something. Look at verse 11," and he pointed to it in his Bible. "Here it says to put on the whole armor of God so that you can *stand against the wiles of the devil*. Now the reverse of that means that if you don't put on the whole armor of God you won't be able to stand against the wiles—the cunning or craftiness or slyness—of the devil. He's a devil full of tricks, Larry, and you need to put on the whole armor of God so you can stand against that."

I nodded. I was experiencing those tricks of the devil, and I had to agree that the devil certainly was cunning and crafty in what he was throwing at me. He went on.

"Now look at verse 13, Larry. It says that you are to take unto you the whole armor of God that you might be able to stand in the evil day. The evil day is any day when the enemy comes in like a flood."

Well, I certainly know about evil days, I thought, because

the enemy has been coming in like a flood on me these past few weeks.

He continued, "The opposite is also true here. If you don't put on the whole armor of God, you won't be able to stand on those evil days when the enemy rushes in on your life to overwhelm it."

I learned something that day about Ephesians that I hadn't known before. But even more significantly, I began that day to do what the book of Ephesians said to do.

Let me speak to you now as that pastor spoke to me eleven years ago. His two points are crucial for you to consider today. If you don't put on the whole armor of God every day, then you won't be able to take the kingdom by force and you won't win the race you're running. You'll be tripped up by the enemy coming in like a flood over you. You won't be able to stand against the cunning of the devil.

You've Got to Dress for Success

A number of self-help books on the market today advocate what they call "dressing for success." These authors believe that a certain "look" will help a person achieve more and have a better reputation in the business world.

Dressing for success is a reality as well in the spiritual realm, and it involves putting on the whole armor of God. In fact, that's the only way to dress for success in the Lord, because the whole armor of God is a prerequisite to taking the kingdom of God by force, winning the race and withstanding the enemy in evil days. So you've got to learn to put on the whole armor of God, and do it every day.

Who exactly is to put on the whole armor of God? Verse 10 of this chapter starts out with the answer: "Finally, my brethren."

People often say, "I don't think I can do that. Putting on the whole armor of God means I need to remember a lot of Scripture. I can't remember that much." Then they try to justify themselves by saying, "That's only for preachers."

I don't agree with them. When my son was only four years old, he could put on the whole armor of God in just the way I'm about to tell you. So I don't buy that excuse.

Putting on the whole armor of God is for anyone who wants to overcome. It's not just for preachers. It's for "the brethren."

Of course, if you're one of those who say, "Win some, lose some, and some get rained out," then this strategy isn't for you. So don't bother with excuses; just be honest with yourself and say, "I don't care about winning over the devil. I don't care about what he does to me. So I don't need to know this." If you're one of the "brethren," however, one who wants to win the race and take what God has for you to receive, then putting on the whole armor of God is critical to you.

I want to point out especially that this is called the armor of God. Why? Because Jesus Christ Himself wore it! In Isaiah 59:15-18 we read:

> Then the Lord saw...that there was no justice. He saw that there was no man, and wondered [which means He was amazed] that there was no intercessor; therefore His own arm brought salvation for Him; and His own righteousness, it sustained Him. For He put on righteousness as a breastplate, and a helmet of salvation on His head; He put on the garments of vengeance for clothing, and was clad with zeal as a cloak.

This is a prophetic word from Isaiah about Jesus. He was the first one to wear the "armor of God" described by Paul in his letter to the Ephesians.

But why did Jesus need the armor of God? Because He had divested Himself of His heavenly privileges and was living out His life on the earth in human, bodily form, encountering the same types of circumstances and situations that you and I face today. Philippians 2:7-8 says that Jesus "made Himself of no reputation, taking the form of a servant, and coming in the likeness of men. And being found in appearance as a man, He humbled Himself and became obedient to the point of death, even the death of the cross."

As a man, Jesus chose to be clothed with this "armor of God" in order to live out His life in obedience and victory on this earth. How much more so, then, do you and I need this same armor!

What is this armor? It's the very character and attributes of God Himself. As we go through these pieces of armor and learn what they mean and how to put them on, turn your attention to one central fact: Each piece of armor is nothing more than a manifestation of the Lord Jesus Christ in our lives. We're really putting on Jesus Christ—and the character traits manifested by Him, which were a reflection of the character of God Himself—as our defense and our offense while we live out our lives in this world. We're talking about a way of releasing the character of Jesus Christ so that the One who is on the inside of us can be manifest on the outside of us.

Do you have Jesus living on the inside of you? Then "putting on the whole armor of God" is a way for you to actualize or to manifest the Lord Jesus Christ in an outward way.

Jesus Is the Whole Armor of God

Let's discover Jesus in these pieces of armor listed in Ephesians. First, in verse 14: We are to have our "waist girded with truth." Who is your truth? It is Jesus Christ. He Himself said, "I am the way, the truth and the life" (John 14:6).

Next, in the same verse in Ephesians: "having put on the

95

breastplate of righteousness." Who is your righteousness? It is Jesus Christ. You have no righteousness of your own. Only the blood of Jesus covering you gives you the gift of righteousness, which is Jesus Himself.

In verse 15: "feet shod with the preparation of the gospel of peace." What is that preparation of the gospel of peace? The gospel is that Jesus Christ died for our sins, according to the Scriptures, was buried, and rose again the third day. The word preparation means "readiness" to walk in the gospel of peace. It's the ability to walk in the Spirit of God just as Jesus did.

In verse 16: "taking the shield of faith." Who is your faith? Nobody but Jesus! Who else produces faith in your life?

Many people think that faith is some kind of mental exercise or something they need to work themselves into. But no—faith is the ability to submit yourself to the lordship of Christ, so that, as you take in the Word of God, the Spirit of God comes into your heart and produces faith to believe for the things of God.

I like what the apostle Paul said when he wrote, "It's not I, but Christ that lives. And the life I now live I live· by the faith of the Son of God" (Gal. 2:20). Read it again· the faith of the Son of God. Jesus Christ has produced that faith which is now in your life.

In verse 17 of Ephesians 6: "take the helmet of salvation." Who is your salvation today? Jesus Christ.

In the same verse: "the sword of the Spirit, which is the word of God." Who is the Word of God? Jesus Christ. John 1:1-2 says, "In the beginning was the Word, and the Word was with God and the Word was God. He was in the beginning with God." John is talking about His Master and Lord, Jesus Christ.

Putting on the "whole armor of God," then, is really putting on the "whole of Jesus." It's appropriating who Jesus is and what Jesus has done. It's putting on Jesus so that He can work in and through our lives. It's Jesus *in* us, Jesus *through* us and Jesus *for* us.

How Do You Put on the Whole Armor of God?

Putting on the armor of God is based on this three-part principle: 1) God gave the promise. 2) Jesus said, "Yes." 3) We say, "Amen!"

Second Corinthians 1:20 says, "All the promises of God are in him, yea, and to us, amen." God promised that Jesus would be our truth. Jesus said yes to that promise of God. Then we say amen to it—or "so be it in my life." That's what "amen" means—"so be it in my life."

When we say amen to Jesus as our truth, we are actually releasing Jesus Christ to be truth in our inner man. To actualize or to bring to reality anything in the spiritual realm means to do two things: first, to believe in your heart that it is so, and second, to confess what you believe with your mouth.

You say, "I believe Jesus is in me. I believe He is the truth. I believe that He is the truth in me. I believe it in my heart."

God gave that promise. Jesus is saying by His living Spirit, "Yes, that's right. I am the truth; I was the truth; I will be the truth. I am the truth in your life right now." All I need to do, then, is say, "Amen! I want You to be the truth in my life right now—today." I speak it out. I declare it to be.

God gave the promise. Jesus says, "Yes." You say, "Amen!" That's how you put on the armor of God, piece-by-piece.

The Girdle of Truth

The first piece of armor is described as our "waist girded with truth." In another translation it says, "loins girt about with truth." What exactly is that waist covering? What are your "loins"?

Your loins are those secret parts of the body—your reproductive organs and the organs that dispel waste. In the spiritual realm, then, you're appropriating truth to release the spiritual waste—or falsehood, lies, deceit—out of your life. And you're appropriating truth so that you're ready to reproduce yourself in God.

How do you put on that girdle of truth? Here's how I put it on every day. I stand before God in prayer and say: "God, in the name of Jesus, I know that You are the truth and You are in me, and I say amen today that You are my truth. I want You as truth in me."

Then I know that Jesus is my truth for this day. I get a mental picture of a big girdle or belt coming over my loins.

The Breastplate of Righteousness

Next I stand before the Lord and say, "God, You gave me as a free gift my righteousness, which is the blood of Jesus." Then I see in my mind's eye that big breastplate coming over my chest to cover my heart and lungs.

Now my heart pumps blood to my body in the natural, and the Scriptures teach that "life is in the blood." (See Deut. 12:23.) The same thing is true spiritually. My Jesus heart pumps blood to my entire life, and my spiritual life is in the blood of Jesus. My spiritual lungs allow me to breathe deeply the Spirit of God. And when those vital organs of my body are spiritually covered with the righteousness of God, then I can breathe the fresh sweet air of God's Holy Spirit and experience His life in a way that activates and energizes my entire being.

Do you know what it means to breathe smoggy air, spiritually speaking? Do you know what it means to have a shortness of spiritual breath? Do you know what it means to have heart palpitations or blood vessel constrictions of the spirit?

Shortly before I was born again in 1968, I went through a traumatic time. I experienced a nervous breakdown to the extent that I was hospitalized. One of the symptoms of my condition during that time was that I couldn't take a deep breath. My breathing was shallow because I was so anxious over my life.

I wasn't walking with God; I didn't have the Spirit of God in my life at that time; I wasn't experiencing the peace, joy and righteousness of God. That condition will make any person anxious. It's amazing to me that more people who don't know God aren't hospitalized with nervous breakdowns.

But once I was born again and a healing took root in my life, I could breathe deeply. So I can tell you from experience that if you haven't been able to breathe deeply, taking a deep breath is one of the greatest feelings you can ever have.

The same is true in the spiritual realm. When you know that you're covered with the breastplate of the righteousness of God, which is your gift through the blood of Jesus Christ, then your heart pumps its spiritual vitality freely to all parts of your being. The constrictions dissolve because you aren't struggling to make your own life right before God according to your works or performance. The pace of your life evens out because you aren't struggling to achieve righteousness on your own.

When you aren't struggling to achieve your own righteousness, you can breathe deeply those things of the Spirit of God. You can take them into your being with freedom, breathing all the way down and completely filling your spiritual lungs with the breath of God.

The Gospel of Peace

Jesus is ready to walk in the right paths. He's living on the inside of me. He's prepared to walk after the Spirit and not after the flesh.

That's what verse 15 in Ephesians 6 says: "having shod your feet with the preparation of the gospel of peace."

You're to have ever-ready shoes. You're to be prepared to go wherever God sends you, wherever He leads, wherever He directs you.

Are you aware that when you were born again, you received all of the same equipment *spiritually* that you have in the flesh as a result of being born a human being?

For example, you have spiritual ears to hear God's voice. Now a man came to me recently and said, "Do you mean to tell me that you think you hear God talk to you?"

I looked right back and said, "Do you mean to tell me that God doesn't talk to you?"

He said, "What do you mean, 'God talks to you'?"

I said, "Jesus says in my Bible that 'My sheep hear My voice and they follow Me.' It may just be that you are not one of His sheep." (See John 10:27.)

That man probably didn't realize either that we have spiritual taste buds so we can taste and see that the Lord is good (Ps. 34:8). We also have spiritual feet, so that we can walk in the Spirit of God and not fulfill the lust of our flesh (Gal. 5:16).

If I have spiritual feet, then I can stand and say, "God, I know I have Jesus' blood flowing through me, and the Spirit is ready to walk today in Your paths and not into the sins of the flesh. Jesus has said that He would be my preparation. He's saying that He's ready. He's the true ever-ready One." Then I get a knowing deep inside that Jesus is ready to walk out His life through my being and circumstances. And I see boots with His initials coming onto my feet.

During just about every day I come to points where I say, "Well, I'm not sure I'm ready for this, but You're ready, Jesus, so let's go." And that's the way I put on the shoes that prepare me to walk in the gospel of peace. They're not my shoes or my readiness. They are the shoes of Jesus. It's His readiness. And there's nothing—no circumstance or person or demon—that catches Jesus off guard.

I stand amazed at the many self-help books on the secular market that tell us how we can get "righteous"—they don't use that word, but that's what they mean—and how we can get ready for life's challenges. So many of them teach, in effect, that you should get up every morning, look in the mirror and pump yourself up by saying, "Go get 'em, champ. You're going to knock it out of the park today. Smile and keep on smiling. You can do it!"

I'd wear out fast if I had to live that way. I look at myself in the mirror and say, "You can't do this, son. But there's Someone living in you who can. Thank You, Lord, that You're my truth; You're my righteousness; You're my readiness."

The Shield of Faith

Next I take the shield of faith. I stand and say, "God, Jesus is my faith. He is the author and finisher of my faith. He is the source of my faith. And I'm taking Jesus today to lift Him up between me and all the fiery darts the devil tosses my way." Then I see Jesus standing right there between me and the devil and all his demons. He's my invisible shield. And I get a knowing in my knower that He's there in my life to intercept all the stinging words, hurtful temptations, lies and deceitful plots that the devil is about to hurl in my direction. So I say, "Amen!"

Look at verse 16 again: "taking the shield of faith, with which you will be able to quench all the *fiery darts* of the wicked one." The fiery darts are Satan's offense. Your shield of faith, therefore, is your number-one defensive weapon.

Now what are those fiery darts? What are you lifting your shield against? Satan throws at you lies and temptations that are aimed directly at the five-fold covenant you have with God once you're born again by the blood of Jesus. He lies to you:

1) that your sins really aren't forgiven.

2) that you're not really filled with the Holy Spirit, that the Spirit is just an imagination of your mind.

3) that you'll never be healed because God doesn't really want to heal you.

4) that you'll never prosper because God doesn't care about your material well-being.

5) that you'll never be a winner before God or a "conqueror" in life.

Now those are fiery darts! Satan does everything in his power to penetrate your mind with those lies. He's faithful about the task. In fact, the devil is faithful on only one point: He's faithful to come at you with his lies. No, he's not faith-filled. But he's steadfast. And he keeps launching fiery darts in your direction every day without letting up.

How do we fight against those fiery darts? We lift up our shields of faith. We proclaim with our faith just who Jesus is. We proclaim our covenant with God back to Him. We say:

I *am* saved. I've been born again because I've believed on Him just as it says in John 3:16.

I *am* filled with the Holy Spirit of God. I have repented and been baptized, and according to Acts 2:38 I have received the gift of the Holy Ghost.

I *will* be well. God *does* want me healed. He said, "I am the Lord who heals you" and that means me (Ex. 15:26). He was wounded for my transgressions, bruised for my iniquities; the chastisement of my peace was upon Him and by His stripes I *am* healed. (Is. 53:5. See also Matt. 8:17.)

I *will* live in biblical prosperity. God *does* want me to prosper, according to 3 John 2. He wants me to prosper in the same proportion and depth that my soul prospers.

I *will* be a conqueror. God says that I am more than a conqueror through Christ Jesus.

Have you ever had Satan fire a dart at you, telling you that your sins really aren't forgiven and that you aren't saved? Have you ever had Satan fire a dart at you, telling you that you aren't filled with the Holy Spirit because your experience wasn't just like your neighbor's? Have you ever been sick and had Satan fire a dart at you telling you that your sickness will be terminal? Have you ever been out of money and had Satan throw one of his fiery darts at you that says you'll never make it, or you'll probably end up on welfare, or you'll have to declare bankruptcy, or you'll lose your business?

Stop those fiery darts! Lift up your shield of faith and quench them.

Several years ago I flew home from Korea, which is about a twenty-hour trip from Seoul to Dallas by the time you have layovers, refueling and customs. I arrived absolutely exhausted on a Saturday. Then I preached six times on Sunday and conducted a two-day revival on Monday and Tuesday in another city. By Wednesday when I got back home to Dallas my throat had become so swollen that I could hardly talk.

I heard this little voice say in the back of my head, "You know, you ought to take two weeks off. You're tired. You're sick. Make people feel sorry for you. You can get a lot of mileage out of this sore throat."

Whoop! Fiery dart on the way! Time to lift that shield of faith. I said, "Jehovah-rophe, my healer, I will not be sick." And I never missed a day. If I had given into that thing, I probably would have been sick for three months!

The Helmet of Salvation

By the time I get to the helmet of salvation in my prayer time, I'm usually rather happy. So I stand and shout to God with joy, "God, You are my salvation! Thank You, Jesus; You are my salvation!" Then Jesus says, "That's right, boy. I am." And I shout back, "Amen—glory to God, I'm saved!"

If you aren't happy about your salvation—then get saved!

103

Get something down inside you that you know is real. Get something that you know has transformed you from death to life. If you're saved, you have to know it. Otherwise, if you could be saved and not know it, then you could lose it and not miss it. So make sure you know you're saved. And when you know for sure that you've been released from a death sentence and freed forever, I can promise you that you'll be happy.

When I pray this way, I see Jesus putting that helmet of salvation right down over my head. I know I don't have to let anything of the devil into my mind. No imaginations. No daydreams. No stray thoughts. My mind will be the mind of Christ. (See 1 Cor. 2:16.)

The Sword of the Spirit

The sword of the Spirit is the Word of God. So I stand up and say, "God, I thank You that the Word of God, Jesus Christ, is in me. I will walk in that Word today. The words of my mouth and the meditation of my heart will be focused on Your Word, on Your Scriptures, on Your law and commandments, on Your promises, on Your divine majesty."

God gave the promise. Jesus said, "Yes." And I hear Him inside me say, "Yes, I am the Word."

Then I see that sword being put into my hand and I say, "Amen! Let Your Word be my sword today. Let my words be Jesus coming out of me."

How did Jesus defeat the enemy? When Satan came to tempt Jesus in the wilderness (see Matt. 4:1-11), he said, "Turn this stone into bread." Jesus answered him by saying, "Man shall not live by bread alone but by every word that proceeds from the mouth of God."

The enemy came again and said, "Throw Yourself down from the pinnacle of the temple, and the angels shall lift You up before You can hit the ground." Jesus answered, "It is written, you shalt not tempt the Lord your God."

The enemy came a third time and said, "All these things I will give You if You will fall down and worship me." Jesus answered him a third time from the Word: "Away with you, Satan! For it is written, You shall worship the Lord your God and Him only you shall serve."

Jesus was tearing down the strongholds Satan was trying to build up in His mind. He was using the sword of the Scriptures to cut through the darkness of temptations. He used the Word to cut Satan's arguments into shreds.

I like what David said: "I have pursued my enemies...and beat them as fine as the dust of the earth." (Read all about it in 2 Sam. 22:32-51.) Too many of us have spiritual detente with the devil. We say in effect, "You don't mess with me too much and I won't mess with you too much."

Too many people have decided to have what I call a "cruise-matic" Christian walk—laid back and on cruise control. But that won't work. The devil won't quit messing with you. He'll throw detours and roadblocks in your way.

Your offensive weapon to cut through the barricades that Satan has erected is the Word of God. Wield it!

God made the promise. Jesus said, "Yes." And I say, "Amen." Then I order my day according to the Word of God coming out of my mouth.

Pray Always

The final word in this passage from Ephesians is in verse 18: "Praying always with all prayer and supplication in the Spirit." So I keep the prayer flowing all day, both in English and in my language of the Spirit.

The Bible promises that if I'll do that—if I'll put on the armor of God, stand my ground, resist the devil and pray always—then I'll overcome the enemy. I can live in victory. I can win. I can be an overcoming warrior.

Does it work? Yes! I can guarantee you that it does. I've put on the whole armor of God every day for eleven years, and for eleven years I've walked in victory.

I don't walk in victory because I'm a preacher. I know lots of preachers who don't walk in victory. I'm not walking in victory because I don't have problems. Nobody has everything perfect all the time. No, I'm walking in victory because I know who my enemy is and I've learned how to put on my spiritual battle clothes. I put on my armor every day.

We have too many spiritual streakers today. The devil is laughing because they're walking around without their clothes on. Can you imagine a young soldier going off to Vietnam wearing his pajamas? Can you imagine a soldier in World War II storming the beaches of Normandy in his swimsuit? We dare not be that casual or foolish either, as we prepare for battle in the spiritual realm.

The words of the apostle Paul ring in my ears: "Be sober, be vigilant; because your adversary the devil walks about like a roaring lion, seeking whom he may devour. Resist him, steadfast in the faith" (1 Pet. 5:8-9). Be sober. Be vigilant. Watch for him. Be on guard.

Then resist him by standing steadfastly in your faith. Don't allow yourself to be moved from your position of strength in the Lord's might. Be fully dressed for battle. Have your shield in the "ready" position. Have your hand firmly clasped on the sword. Be prepared to march into battle!

Close the Door on the Devil Today

1) Put on the whole armor of God early tomorrow morning. Then at noon, close your eyes for a few seconds and picture in your mind each piece of the armor covering your entire being. Late in the afternoon, close your eyes again for a few seconds and picture yourself completely armed as God's warrior. Then just before you go to bed, close your eyes yet a fourth time and see yourself as a victorious

r these 2 main events real

ur friend & Youth Pastor

rent & Tracy Sheppard
outh Minister
ad Tidings Christian Center

soldier. You have withstood the battle!

2) As you consider your battles, stop to consider the fiery darts you've captured on your shield of faith. What is it that the enemy is trying to throw at you? What are his temptations, his accusations, his threats? Search God's Word with your concordance to come against each one of those fiery darts. Get armed with the Word of God so that you can wield your sword with greater accuracy.

3) Why not write your name in the following blank as a lasting reminder of your commitment to be in God's army?

_____

(Your name here)
Fully Armed Soldier

Let's pray and agree together you'll never forget that the whole armor of God is your best defense and your best offense against the devil: "In the name of Jesus I agree with you that this word is sealed forever in my heart. I declare today that when I am fully armed with the whole armor I have put on Jesus. Therefore the devil must flee when I withstand him, not in my strength, but in the strength of Christ Jesus. I make a new commitment today to put on the whole armor of God every day of my life. Amen."

SEVEN

Marching in the Spirit: Choosing Praise

Imagine a unit of soldiers marching past, neatly organized into rows, their firearms held just so, their cadence shouted out by the sergeant marching to one side. What exactly is the purpose of their march?

They don't march just for exercise. They're not out just to learn how to walk in neat rows or to know the left foot from the right. No—the purpose of marching is to move a unit of soldiers as efficiently and quickly as possible from one battlefield to the next. When an enemy shot is fired and the man in charge cries, "Fall in!" a good soldier knows to grab his weapon immediately and get into line. Then the soldiers march together—or even run together—to the designated spot. They move as a unit and their rows and cadence help keep them together as a fighting body.

As a soldier in God's army today you are part of the fighting body of Christ. You'll experience battles, and in between those battles you'll find there's a whole lot of marching to be done. The Scriptures tell us to "walk in the Spirit" (Gal. 5:25), but because we're part of God's army, I like to speak of "marching in the Spirit."

As God's soldiers, how do we "march in the Spirit"? How do we move as the body of Christ from one battle to the next, arriving prepared and ready to take on the enemy?

First of all, we have to clear up some common misconceptions. The first misconception is that many folks seem to think that after you've been born again, all your problems should be solved. You just automatically march in the Spirit and you never have another trial.

But that's not the way it is. It's *after* you're born again—after you've come to Christ, repented of your sins, received His forgiveness and been filled with the Holy Spirit—that you learn how to walk in victory. Problems and troubles won't disappear just because you've become a Spirit-filled Christian. You're still in this world.

The average citizen on the street doesn't learn to march—the soldier does. The soldier is the one given marching orders about what to do when troubles arise.

A second misconception about the Christian life is this: Walking in the victory of the Holy Spirit is only for an elite group of superspiritual people. Not so! Walking in victory, walking in the Spirit, marching as part of the body of Christ with a warrior mentality to take on the enemy, is for every believer, including you.

No one is exempt from drills in a military boot camp. If you qualify to enlist or to be drafted into the armed services, you must be capable of marching. Furthermore, you must participate whether you feel like it or not, whether you want to or not, whether the blisters on your feet are ready to or not. And unless you're in the infirmary, when the sergeant calls out, "Fall in!" you'd better fall in, and fall in quickly. Everyone learns to march: the seaman, the pilot, the medic, the computer operator, as well as the foot soldier.

The same is true for the army of God. The Lord intends for everyone to live in victory and to march in the Spirit. But how is it done?

Don't Worry

Philippians 4:6-7 says, "Be anxious for nothing, but in everything by prayer and supplication, with thanksgiving, let your requests be made known unto God, and the peace of God, which surpasses all understanding, will guard your hearts and minds through Christ Jesus."

"Be anxious for nothing" might be best translated into our terms today as "Don't worry about anything." So the eleventh commandment for the folks in our church is "thou shalt not sweat it." That might sound irreverent to you, but the message is the same as what the apostle Paul wrote to the church at Philippi: Don't live full of worry. You must make a decision not to dwell on your problems.

Of course, that doesn't mean you won't have any problems. Jesus said, "In this world you will have tribulation" (John 16:33). The world is full of problems, and in today's high-pressure society especially, no one is exempt from stress.

The pressures and problems of our life-style today are typified by the plight of a motorist in rush-hour traffic on the freeway. Everyone is trying to get home as quickly as possible. Cars are whizzing by one another at sixty miles per hour or more, changing lanes, turning onto entrance and exit ramps—and making these high-speed maneuvers with only a few feet between them. At any second something could go wrong to cause a terrible collision.

Many of these pressures don't even enter our conscious minds. We just experience them and internalize them so that they become a part of the clutter in our inner person. Then we wonder why we're so tense and tired all the time.

The first thing we must do, then, to walk victoriously in the Spirit is to make a conscious decision that we will not dwell on the problems around us.

I recently talked to a married couple who had a serious problem in their home. I said, "First of all, let's not worry

111

about this. Let's choose *not* to fret about this.''

But the wife said to me, ''Well, if I'm not going to worry about it, what do you want me to do about it?''

Worry is a natural first reaction when we experience trouble. Our human instinct is to get nervous and anxious about the situation, to try figuring out with our minds what to do first. But I believe that the first thing we're to do when we're faced with a problem is to pull ourselves up short and say, ''I will not worry about this.''

That may sound like simply denying the reality of the situation, but it's not. I'm not saying that the problem doesn't exist, that the trouble isn't a real trouble. Nor am I saying that you should stick your head in the sand and pretend the problem isn't there.

What I *am* saying is that you have the privilege and authority to determine your response to a real problem. You have the ability to determine your next steps of action rather than wallow in your worry about the situation.

You can and must confront the tendency to worry before worry has time to take root in you. You must recognize the ''worry response'' as the likely first reaction of your natural man to a blow from the enemy. And once you've determined that worry will not consume your time and energy in dealing with the situation, you're in a position to take the next step.

What would happen if, when a group of soldiers heard a missile explode in the distance, they all sat down to wring their hands, saying, ''Oh, poor us. We'll all be killed. We're in big trouble now. Oh, what can we do?'' An army with that kind of response wouldn't win any battles, much less a war.

At the same time, however, a soldier understandably experiences a moment of panic when he hears that missile explode. The danger is present, and it's a real danger. But his strength and training as a soldier compel him to move through that moment of panic to take action. He has been drilled to do something and "not sweat it."

As soldiers in God's army, we too must be trained to move through the panic to the place of action. We must confront worry for what it is—a trick of the enemy that delays us, saps our spiritual energy, stalls our efforts and immobilizes God's people. We must make a conscious, determined decision *not* to worry at the first word of an emergency or a problem.

How do we do that? Choosing not to be anxious doesn't mean that we put our brains in neutral and do nothing. When the apostle Paul told us what *not* to do, he also told us what we *are* to do instead.

Pray About It

Paul told the Philippians not to be anxious, "but in everything by prayer and supplication, with thanksgiving, let your requests be made known unto God" (Phil. 4:6). In short, instead of worrying, start praying.

To me, "prayer" means asking and entreating God, while "supplication" means really getting down to business with God. In supplication, we say, "Lord, I've got to have an answer. I've got to have a solution. And I've got to have Your will on this matter now."

The kind of prayer God hears is a prayer of faith. That's the prayer that says, "God, I believe You knew about this problem even before it came my way." In fact, one of the biblical names for God is Jehovah-jireh, which means "Jehovah, the one who sees."

We find that name in the account of Abraham's attempted sacrifice of Isaac in obedience to God's command (Gen. 22:1-19). The Lord was truly the One who saw everything: He saw Abraham going up the mountain with his son Isaac. He saw the wood they carried. He saw the mental and emotional turmoil going on inside Abraham as he obeyed.

If ever there were a reason to worry, Abraham certainly

had one. But instead we find him going up that mountain saying to himself, "God, Jehovah-jireh, will provide a sacrifice." And he believed that if it was God's will for Isaac to die, then God would raise him from the dead. Abraham had the kind of faith that saw God as the One who would renew life in the resurrection. (See Heb. 11:10.)

So Abraham didn't worry about the situation. He was too busy walking up the mountain. He was too busy believing that God had the situation under control.

Meanwhile, as Abraham and Isaac were walking up one side of the mountain, guess what was happening over on the other side of the mountain? A little ram was already getting itself into position under God's direction. The animal was heading straight for one particular thorn bush, where he would be entangled in exactly the right place at the right time to solve Abraham's problem.

You may be facing a need right now. But let me assure you, God is the One who sees that need at the same time He sees His solution for that need. He is Jehovah-jireh, the One who sees and provides. Just as you're climbing up the mountain in your dilemma and struggle, He's already preparing a ram to solve your problem.

If that's the case, then, how should we pray? We pray according to our covenant with God.

• Jesus has already died to forgive us of our sins. So I can pray that God will forgive me when I repent—or turn around—from the mistakes and sins in my life, accepting Jesus into my life and into any situation or circumstance of my life. So I pray in faith that Jesus will deliver me.

• Jesus has already died so that we can have the fullness of the Holy Spirit. So I can pray that the fullness of the Holy Spirit will be in operation and that I can know His love, joy, peace, patience, faith, mercy, self-control, gentleness and goodness in my life (Gal. 5:22,23). I can pray that the Holy Spirit will be my counselor and my comforter (John 14:16,17).

• Jesus has already died so that we can be healed (Is. 53:5). So I can pray boldly for total health—in body, mind, spirit, relationships and finances (3 John 2). I can pray for wholeness of life.

• Jesus has already died so that we can be "the head and not the tail" (Deut. 28:13). He will be our provider. So I can pray that God will supply my needs and cause me to possess the land He wants me to have.

• Jesus has already died so that we can be more than conquerors and know success in this life (Rom. 8:37). So I can pray that Jesus will rule and reign over any negative circumstances in my life and extend His kingdom to cover that territory and claim it as His own.

Jesus has *already* died for all this! The work has already been done. So victory won't come by anything I do in and of my own efforts. It will come by what I allow Jesus to do in the situation; what I allow Jesus to be in the circumstances; what I allow Jesus to live out, through me, in the midst of the problem.

Many things I simply don't know. I can't know in my finite mind the full will of God. So it's at this point that I must ask for the wisdom of God. I must say, "God, I don't know what to do. But You said in James 1:5 that You'd tell me, that You'd give me superabundant wisdom, if I ask. And You also said that You wouldn't make fun of me for not knowing what to do. So I ask You right now, *what should I do?*"

What do you do when an emergency hits? First, don't worry. Second, start praying according to the five-fold covenant we have with God. Then, as you pray, God will drop faith into your spirit where your faith is weak. He will drop His answer into your heart.

Can you see how impossible it is to experience the faith of God in your heart if you're in a state of worry? You have to get out of worry before you can experience faith. You have to put a stop to one before you can receive the other.

115

Can you see how impossible it is to hear God speak His answer into your heart if you're busy trying to figure things out for yourself in your state of worry? You must get yourself quiet before the Lord and be in an attitude of prayer before you can hear God's voice and understand His will for you in the midst of your circumstances.

Once you hear God's answer—once you feel faith in Him rising up within you—then you're ready for a third step in your "march." This step is critical, because it truly releases the hand of God to move in your circumstances.

Everyone wants to see the hand of God move in their lives. I've never met a person—saved or unsaved—who in their heart of hearts didn't want to see that happen. And the Bible tells us how God's hand moves.

Praise

Philippians 4:7 says to let your requests be made known to God by prayer and supplication *with thanksgiving*. This means that within the circumstances you're experiencing you must start praising and giving thanks to God for the victory you see only by your faith.

Praise is the language of faith. Praise is your way of saying, I acknowledge You, God, as the victor in this circumstance. You are the Lord. You are the king. You are my provider. You are the healer. You are my Savior and deliverer. You are my comforter and my counselor.

Praise is focusing on the outcome of the situation. It's believing and saying with your faith that God wins. To continue the metaphor we used before, if we're a platoon of soldiers marching down the road in God's army, praise is our "sound off": "One, two, three, four, God is gonna' win the war!"

What does the Word of God promise will happen when you move into praise? What will happen when you stop worrying, start praying and voice your thanksgiving to

God? "The peace of God, which surpasses all understanding, will guard your hearts and minds through Christ Jesus" (Phil. 4:7).

Deep, abiding peace is the hallmark of walking in the Spirit. As the psalmist wrote, "He leads me beside the waters" (Ps. 23:2). Show me a man or woman who's walking through life's circumstances with great peace and I'll show you a person who's walking in the victory of the Holy Spirit. I'm not talking about some kind of artificial placidity, where on the outside everything looks calm and under control, but on the inside the pressure is building up and things are about to explode. That's not peace. That's a charade.

I'm not talking either about a man or woman who walks with a dazed look as if all of life is some kind of Sunday school picnic in the park. That's not peace. That's either denial or shell-shock.

I'm talking about true, deep, abiding peace. Jesus said to His disciples on the eve of His crucifixion, "Peace I leave with you. My peace I give to you" (John 14:27). God wants you to have peace.

The Bible says in command form, "Let the peace of God rule in your hearts" (Col. 3:15). To "rule" here means to "umpire" your heart. That means God tells you what is safe and what is out.

Just consider a moment what comes after a battle and ultimately after a war: peace. Walking in the victory of the Holy Spirit is knowing that while there may be a battle, you'll win because of Jesus inside you. It's knowing that peace will be established and declaring the outcome even in advance of taking any action or confronting the enemy.

As soon as you declare the praises of God, God activates the solution to your problem, the supply for your lack, the answer for your dilemma. All of heaven gets to work on the problem the minute you start praising.

In 2 Chronicles 20 we read about a terrible mess

Jehoshaphat found himself in. He was completely surrounded by the children of Ammon and Moab and the inhabitants of Mount Seir. He was invaded from three sides by the combined forces of the enemy.

The Bible says that Jehoshaphat "set himself to seek the Lord" (2 Chr. 20:3). He didn't set himself to worry. He had a real problem and he knew it. But he made up his mind that he would seek the Lord.

I can't imagine anyone reading this book who has a bigger problem than Jehoshaphat had in that moment when three alien armies were on his borders and there was no apparent way of escape. Yet in the face of such an overwhelming problem, he prayed the covenant promises of God. He prayed, "God, You gave us this land. This is our land but it is only ours because You provided it for us and gave it to us. You are the ruler of this land. And now we're about to be overrun by the enemy. We could have destroyed these people when we first came into this area but You told us not to do that, and now we're about to be invaded by these people."

Notice what Jehoshaphat said next to the Lord: "Lord, we don't know what to do." That's not a bad place to be before God. There's nothing wrong with coming to God in an attitude of not knowing.

Then Jehoshaphat added, "But...our eyes are upon You." He didn't have an answer and he knew it. He hadn't been to college to earn a degree in how to defeat these armies. He hadn't been in this position before so he couldn't rely on past experience. He didn't know what at all to do.

Nevertheless Jehoshaphat did know Someone who had the answer. He knew where to put his eyes. So "all Judah with their little ones, their wives, and their children, stood before the Lord." The whole group came together before God to see what God would say to do (2 Chr. 20:13).

What happened next? Jehoshaphat got an answer about what to do. I've never seen it fail: When a person begins

118

to pray the covenant, saying to God, "I don't know what to do in this situation but my eyes are on You," an answer comes every time.

If you come to God and tell Him how bad your problems are, you'll probably never hear an answer from God because you'll never get around to asking Him the question. You'll be too busy reciting the circumstances. But if you come to God and pray the Word of God back to Him, God always responds to His Word.

The answer God sent came through Jahaziel, who was the son of somebody, who was the son of somebody else— four generations of Jahaziel's family are mentioned. They knew who this Jahaziel was precisely. As Jahaziel stood, the Spirit of the Lord came in the midst of the congregation and said through him, in effect, "Listen, everybody. The Lord says to you, 'Don't be afraid or dismayed. The battle isn't yours, but God's. Go down to where they are tomorrow. But you won't need to fight in this battle. Position yourselves, stand your ground, and see the salvation of the Lord. Don't be afraid, for the Lord will be with you.' "

Jehoshaphat bowed his head to the ground and all the people fell before the Lord, worshipping Him. They started their praise service! The Bible says, "They stood up to praise the Lord God of Israel with loud and high voices" (2 Chr. 20:19). They got happy before God—even with those three great armies camped all about them.

The next morning Jehoshaphat gathered all the people together and said, "Listen, everybody. Believe in the Lord your God, and you will be established. Believe His prophets and you will prosper."

Then he gathered the choir together and told them, "You will march on the enemy, but not with man-made weapons of warfare. You will lead the way with spiritual weapons of warfare. You will march declaring the high praises of God and singing praises to the Lord."

The Bible says, "When they began to sing and to praise, the Lord set ambushments against the children of Ammon, Moab, and mount Seir." Notice that it doesn't say God began to act after they finished their song, but when they *began* to sing. That's Jehovah-jireh in action once again. He sees the beginning from the end. He already had the plan figured out. He was just waiting for them to push the "start" button with their praises.

What happened next? The enemy became so confused that they began killing one another. The soldiers of Ammon and Moab started fighting the inhabitants of Mount Seir. Then after they had slain them, they turned on one another until, the Scriptures say, "they helped to destroy one another" (2 Chr. 20:23).

It took Jehoshaphat and the people three days to gather up all the spoil. They found an abundance of riches and precious jewels. In fact, it was more than they could carry away. They had prospered in the face of an enemy assault. So Jehoshaphat renamed the valley "Berachah," which means "the valley of blessing."

He had decided that instead of worrying, he would pray the covenant. Then the Lord dropped faith and direction into the people's hearts and they stood to praise God. Finally, out of praise, great victory came to pass.

Perhaps you're thinking, But Jehoshaphat was in the will of God, and forces beyond his control came against him. My problems are self-induced. I'm not facing three armies from a foreign land. I've made mistakes and created my own mess.

If that's the case, I have good news for you. It's found in the story of a prophet by the name of Jonah.

God told Jonah, "Go down and preach at Nineveh." Jonah responded by fleeing from the presence of the Lord. That's first-class disobedience, and any time you sin or are disobedient to God, you're fleeing from God's face.

Jonah went down to Joppa, the Scripture says. And

wherever you may run, you always go *down* when you disobey.

Jonah paid the fare and got on a boat in Joppa. When you disobey and flee from God, there are always dues to pay.

The boat was headed for Tarshish, and as they sailed, a great wind arose at God's hand. There will always be a storm surrounding you when you disobey God, when God tells you to do one thing and you choose to do the opposite. And when that storm is the result of your disobedience, you'll know it. Others may not figure it out, but you'll know.

Jonah was asleep down in the hold of that ship. So the others on board came to him and said, "How can you sleep? Get up and call on God. One of us has obviously done something wrong to bring about this great storm. Let's cast lots to see who it is."

The lot fell to Jonah. They said, "What did you do wrong?"

Jonah answered, "I'm a prophet of the God that made heaven, earth and this sea, and I have disobeyed God and fled from His presence."

They asked, "What can we do to remedy the situation?"

He said, "Just throw me overboard." Jonah was ready to die. He was so low about his circumstances that he didn't care what happened to him. And sometimes we feel that way as well—the problem is so great that we really don't care what happens. So like Jonah, we end up in the storm-tossed waves of the sea.

Yet Jehovah-jireh was at work in Jonah's life just as He is in ours. The God who sees saw Jonah go down to Joppa. He saw Jonah get on the boat that set sail for Tarshish. He saw a great fish in another part of the sea. And He called the fish. The Bible says God spoke to that great fish to be in the precise position where it needed to be when Jonah was thrown overboard. So the great fish swallowed Jonah.

What did Jonah do once he found himself in the belly of that fish? He decided to get his mind off his problem.

Now that was a mighty big decision! He was down there in that smelly, dark, confining, frightening place. But Jonah chose as an act of his will not to worry, but rather to pray His covenant promises. He prayed, "Lord, You said if we would worship toward Your holy temple, then the Lord our God would be mighty. So I'm giving to You, God, what already belongs to You—my life and my soul. I'm giving it to You with thanksgiving. I'm giving my will to You to make good what I have vowed. I'm trusting You for salvation, for salvation comes from You, Lord."

Then suddenly that fish got a sour stomach, and he got sick of Jonah. Your problems will also get sick of you when you begin to pray your covenant blessings in the midst of your circumstances rather than worry about them. Then, like Jonah, you'll find yourself on dry ground.

If you're feeling that you've caused the problems that surround you, the circumstances can still change. Don't worry about them; pray about them. Repent of your disobedience and turn your entire life back over to God. Start praying His covenant promises. Begin to praise God in the very midst of your circumstances, and I believe that you too will see the salvation—the deliverance—of the Lord.

Jehoshaphat's problems were external and unprovoked. Jonah's problems were self-induced and rooted in disobedience. But what about problems that come about because of something you've done right?

Jesus said in the Sermon on the Mount that we can be persecuted for righteousness' sake. (See Matt. 5:10.) That doesn't make the pain any less or the circumstances any easier. But at least we know we're not the only ones to have it happen.

Remember Paul and Silas? They were put in jail for doing something *right*. They were walking down the street on their way to a prayer meeting, and a little demon-possessed girl was following them. She was saying the right thing but she didn't have the right spirit. She cried out, "These men are the servants of the Most High God, who proclaim to us the way of salvation" (Acts 16:17).

She followed them for days until Paul finally had enough of her nonsense. He turned and said to the demon in her, "I command you in the name of Jesus Christ to come out of her." And it came out!

Now the men who were making money from her demonic ability to tell fortunes became extremely angry at that point. So they incited a mob and brought the magistrates in. As a result Paul and Silas were nearly beaten to death. Then they were thrown into the inner prison where their hands and feet were bound in stocks.

Can you imagine how Silas in particular must have felt? This was his first missionary trip. He no doubt had thought that once he was out on the road with the apostle Paul, they'd have their van and their albums and their bundles of tracts. He probably figured that by now they'd be on closed circuit television because of overflow crowds in the largest auditoriums they could rent.

But instead Silas found himself nearly beaten to death with his hands and feet in chains, next to the apostle Paul who was in exactly the same condition. Then Paul dared to say, "Don't worry about this, Silas. This just goes with the territory. I'll tell you what—let's sing a few choruses to God."

There they were at midnight—the least likely time to start singing—with nobody around to pat them on the back and encourage them in their faith. But observe what happened.

First, they prayed. (See Acts 16:25.)

Second, they sang praises to God. In fact, they sang so loud that all the other prisoners heard them. They weren't just humming a few bars to themselves. They were belting out those songs.

Then, the Bible says, "*suddenly* there was a great earth-quake...and *immediately* their chains were loosed and the doors flung open."

Now I don't believe Paul and Silas prayed a griping prayer that came out of worry. I believe Paul and Silas prayed, "Thank You, Lord, that I've been given the privilege of suffering for Your name. I'm a servant of the most high God and I believe the hand of the Lord is on my life, even in this prison."

I don't believe that Paul and Silas started singing, "Farther along, we'll know all about it...." I believe they sang, "Bless the Lord, O my soul, and all that is within me, bless His holy name!"

Jehovah-jireh, the God who sees, saw Paul and Silas on their way to the prayer meeting. He saw their encounter with that demon-possessed girl. He saw the way they were treated by the owners of that girl, the crowds and the magistrates. He saw them there in that prison. And He saw the outcome, too.

God was just waiting for those praises to start bouncing off the walls and down the hallways of that dark dungeon in Philippi. And when the praise rolled out of the mouths of Paul and Silas, all of heaven went on active alert! The circumstances changed suddenly, immediately—not three weeks later. Not "down the road." But immediately God's hand was invoked and something happened. Out of it came salvation and deliverance, not only for Paul and Silas, but for a jailer's entire family, and probably many others in that prison.

When those chains fell off his wrists, Silas was probably saying, "Let's get out of here!" But Paul was in no hurry. He knew they were about to have an evangelistic meeting right then and there. He knew the Philippian church was being formed.

You have pressures and problems today, no matter who you are or how long you've been following Jesus Christ as the king of your life. Your troubles may have come totally from the outside, as Jehoshaphat's did. They may be problems that you caused, as were Jonah's. They may be problems that came about because of something you did right in God's eyes, as in the case of Paul and Silas. And though you may not face an enemy army, or a storm at sea, or a dark prison cell, your circumstances are just as real, just as painful, just as terrifying to you.

In the midst of that situation you have a choice to make. You can choose to worry or you can choose *not* to worry. So choose not to worry.

You can choose to pray or not to pray. So choose to pray. With all prayer and supplication before God let your requests be made known. Repent of your past and the mistakes you have made. Pray your covenant with God: that He is your salvation; that the Holy Spirit is your comforter and your counselor; that He is your healer; that He is your provider; that He is more than a conqueror in you.

Finally, you can choose to praise God or not to praise. So choose to praise God!

When you pray instead of worrying; when you experience faith rising in your heart and God's words of direction come to you as a result of prayer; and when you begin to praise God on the basis of who He is and what He will do in your circumstances—something happens. God will move on your behalf!

Your feet are placed solidly on the path of peace. You start walking with your head high, your shoulders thrown back and a joyful smile on your face. You're in a position to look around and see your circumstances change completely for your good—changed by almighty God, Jehovah-jireh, who sees your beginning from your end and knows exactly where you are and what you need.

Are you ready to start marching in the victory of the Spirit today? I believe you are, and I believe you will!

Close the Door on the Devil Today

1) What is the foremost problem you are facing (a situation, an event, a bad memory about the past, a doubt, a person)? List as many as you wish.

2) Now go back and next to each item write down a Scripture verse that declares what God says about the problem. Use a concordance to locate relevant verses that get to the heart of God's opinion about the matter.

3) Pray the covenant over your list of worries. Declare that you are forgiven. Declare that you will know the fullness of the Holy Spirit operating in your life. Declare that you are healed. Declare that God will provide all your needs. Declare that you are a conqueror!

4) Begin to praise God for victory as you cross a line through each one of your worries, declaring what you believe God is going to do in every situation, circumstance or area of your life.

5) Why not write your name in the blank below as a lasting reminder that you are making a commitment to choose prayer and praise over worry?

_____

(Your name here)
Former Worrier
Current Prayer and Praise Warrior

Let's pray and agree together you'll never forget that you must trade in worry for prayer and praise: "In the name of Jesus, I agree with you that this word is sealed forever in my heart. I declare today that I will pray instead of worry. I will praise You, Lord, for Your victory. Help me to confront every worry quickly and decisively with prayer, beginning right now. Amen."

EIGHT

Our Battle Cry:
A Good Testimony

The Philistine army had gathered on one mountain range, and the armies of King Saul on another. Between them lay a great valley.

Every morning for forty days, Goliath, the champion of the Philistines, had come out onto the plain and stood there defiantly, shouting a challenge to Saul and his mighty men: "Send out a man so we can fight together. If he wins, we will be your servants. But if I win, you will be our servants."

Day after day the challenge came. But the story in 1 Samuel 17 tells us that Saul and his men had become dismayed and afraid. Fear was reigning in the camp, not faith. Gloom filled the atmosphere, not joy. The Israelites believed their enemy would win, and that belief was at the root of their fear.

There stood Goliath, six cubits and a span tall—about nine feet nine inches! He was dressed for battle. His helmet was brass. His coat of armor, or "breastplate," weighed 157 pounds. In addition, he was wearing brass leggings and an extra piece of brass across his chest. The point of his huge spear was made of nearly nineteen pounds of iron. He was an awesome fighting machine—in the natural.

Each day as Goliath bellowed out his challenge, "Send

me someone to fight,'' his voice echoed out across the plain and up into the mountains. There the great soldiers of Saul quaked in their boots, scuffed the ground in front of them and said, ''Not me, please.''

Now a man named Jesse had three boys in that army, and since his sons had been away for over a month, Jesse got a bit worried about how they were doing and whether they had enough to eat. So he called his youngest son, David, in from the fields where he had been taking care of the family's sheep. He told the boy: ''Son, take your brothers some of this dried corn and some loaves of bread and these hunks of cheese, and see how they're doing up there in Shochoh.''

Then David found someone to take care of the sheep for him and he set out. Meanwhile, Saul had positioned his armies for battle and the Philistines had positioned themselves as well. So you can just imagine David as he came riding up right into the midst of this battleground, unaware of what was going on. I can see him as he got out of his chariot, found his brothers and said, ''Hi, brothers. What's happening?''

Just at that time, Goliath, that massive henchman of the Philistines, came out from among the armies and stood there in all of his armor, shouting, ''Send me a man!'' And when this giant of a man stepped forward, everybody in the Israelite army took a giant step backward.

When David saw what was happening, he said to his brothers and the other soldiers, ''What's the reward for killing this guy?''

They told him, ''The man who can defeat this Philistine giant named Goliath will get three things: great riches, the king's daughter as a wife [which would make the winning soldier a part of the royal family], and the status of freedom for the winning soldier's family [which meant no taxes and no enslavement of any kind, including no draft into the army].'' Now that was like a *guaranteed* winning of a multimillion-dollar sweepstakes prize. But King Saul had no takers.

So David said, "Well, why aren't you guys doing something about this?"

They answered, "Who are you with your bright ideas? You're just a smart-mouthed young kid straight from the farm who wants to see somebody go out there and get butchered."

David figured he must have asked the wrong group of men so he asked another group, "Why aren't you doing something?" And they answered him the same way. So David said to them all, "This is a cause worth fighting for; why don't you fight?" He stirred up conviction—and trouble. (They often go together.)

Eventually word about David got around to King Saul, so he called for the boy. When David walked into the king's tent he said, "King, I don't understand this. This guy's not worth anybody getting scared over. I'll go fight him."

King Saul must have smiled. Here was an inexperienced kid from the farm who had never been a soldier and was not even full-grown yet. So the king said, "You're not able to go out there. You're not even a man yet. And this guy has been a trained soldier from the time he was a boy." (Can you imagine how big Goliath must have been even as a child? He was probably six feet tall in the third grade!)

David said, "Well, maybe I'm not trained as a soldier. But I'm a pretty good shot with a sling. And I've already killed with my bare hands both a lion and a bear who tried to steal our sheep. Surely the same God who delivered me from a roaring lion and a powerful bear can deliver me from this guy who's defying God's people."

So Saul said, "All right, if that's the case, maybe you are our man. Here, take my suit of armor." And King Saul tried to suit up David in man-made armor.

But that was a mistake. Goliath was suited up in *man-made* armor and King Saul tried to send David out in *man-made* armor. But the battle was really a *spiritual* battle.

I believe it took David about sixty seconds of wearing that man-made pile of metal before he said, "This won't work. I don't know how to wear this suit or use this sword."

So he took off that man-made armor, took up his staff, chose five smooth stones from the river bed and put them in his little shepherd's bag. Then he took up his sling and said, "I'll just go like this, thank you." He set out down the mountainside, and all along the way, he was putting on his *spiritual* armor.

I can just hear David as he went down that mountainside. "I've got on the breastplate of Your righteousness, Jehovah. I've got on Your helmet. I've got on Your protection for my loins. I've got on Your shoes. I've got Your sword and Your shield. I'm a soldier of God. I've got on God's armor. I'm wearing the Lord from head to toe."

When he got out there on the plain and came toward Goliath, the giant looked down at him—from way up there nine feet above the earth—and his eyes took in this lightweight teenager who didn't even have a beard yet. He roared with laughter and swore at him, saying, "What an insult to have them send someone like you! You're about to be fed to the birds!"

Now that moment was a make-or-break point for David. David could have run away and no one would have thought much about it. His brothers and their friends up in the mountains would probably have said, "See, we told you so," and had a good laugh; but deep down inside, they wouldn't have held it against David because they were afraid themselves.

But if he had turned back, something would have happened inside David. He would have known that he had failed before God.

Instead, something took hold inside David in that

moment. A warrior mentality rose in him; a pressing-toward-the-mark faith began to mount up.

David said, "Look here, Philistine. You're coming at me with all your man-made weapons—your sword and spear and shield. But I've got on the armor of God. I'm coming to you in the name of the Lord of hosts, the God of the armies of Israel. This day the Lord will deliver you into my hand. I'll kill you, Goliath, and cut off your head. Not only that, all those armies behind you will be defeated and left to rot out here in the plain to feed the birds and wild animals. The whole world will know about the God of Israel! Everybody here will know that the Lord saves *not* with sword or spear, but by His power. This battle is the Lord's, and He will give you into our hands."

Can't you hear that echo as it rolled back through the hills of Israel and through the camp of the Philistines on the other side of the valley?

The battle is the Lord's, and He will give you into our hands.

The battle is the Lord's, and He will give you into our hands.

The battle is the Lord's, and He will give you into our hands.

I believe that as that shout of victory echoed, faith took root in the hearts of those soldiers of Israel, driving out their fear. I believe they stood a little bit taller in that moment. Something happened. It may not have been visible, but in the spiritual realm, the tide was turning at that very moment.

At the same time, I believe, a seed of doubt and fear took root in the heart of Goliath. He considered for just an instant, "Maybe this kid is right."

Now the Bible says that David *ran* toward Goliath. He didn't inch his way into the situation; he didn't stick one toe into the water to test it first; he didn't back into the battle. He went running flat out toward this

131

foe of God almighty.

As he was running, he got a stone from his bag, put it into his sling and started to whirl it around his head. In those few seconds with David coming at him full speed, his slingshot whirling, Goliath must have had a split-second of knowing, *This isn't what I had in mind.*

Can't you just see David running toward Goliath, his arm whirling that sling and shouting at the top of his lungs, "The battle is the Lord's and He will give you into our hand!" This was do or die. This was putting it all on the line.

So David let that stone fly straight at Goliath's forehead, and the stone sank in, stunning the giant so that he fell with a great thud to the ground. Since David had no sword, he ran up to Goliath, took the man's sword and used it to whack off the giant's head.

When the Philistines saw what had happened, they turned tail and ran for all they were worth. The soldiers of Saul gave a mighty victory shout and came running down from the hills. They had become electrified by what David had done and they pursued the Philistines all the way to the gates of the nearest city, killing and wounding thousands of them as they went. When the battle was won, they went back and cleaned up the spoil from the Philistine tents. The battle was won in a day, ending a war that had been at a stalemate for weeks.

Does David's story sound anything like your own? Of course, you may not be facing an armored giant and an enemy host in the natural sense. In your case, it may be that the bills are piled up, the doctor's diagnosis isn't hopeful, or the problems with your child or spouse seem never-ending. Perhaps day after day the devil and all his hosts call out to you, "So you want to fight? Well, come on out. If I defeat you, you'll be my slave. You'll be forever held in bondage to this situation of poverty, sickness and despair."

No matter who you are, I doubt that everything is perfect

in your life, your family, your church, your workplace. In some area of life, you're bound to face trouble, because there's a war going on.

The sides are divided up: God's people are on one side; the devil and his host of demons are on the other. The enemy is sending trouble out on the plain to shout at you in defiance, "Come on out and fight, you scaredy-cat! I dare you. I double-dare you. You call yourself a Christian and yet you won't even lift a finger to come out here and fight!"

Meanwhile, most of us Christians are hiding up in the hills of our lives, too scared to move. We don't have a fighting mentality. We don't have the mind-set of a warrior. We're saying to ourselves, "If I just lay low, this will pass. Don't ask me to go out on that plain and confront this trouble."

We don't rise up and say, "This shouldn't be happening to me as God's child. This shouldn't be happening to God's people or to God's church." We aren't saying as David said, "This is a godly cause! How dare the devil defy us in this way! How dare he insult our God!"

No, we're sitting up in the hills keeping our mouths shut. We refuse to put on the armor of God and run toward our problems with the full force of our faith, shouting in our inner man as we go, "I'm coming at you, trouble, in the name of the Lord of hosts. I'm coming at you in the name of God almighty, in whose army I'm a soldier. Devil, what you're doing is an insult to my God, and I won't take it any more. I won't listen to your threats. You and your demons will be utterly destroyed on this battlefield of my life, and everyone will see the power of God at work. You're coming at me to destroy me in the natural, but I'm coming at you to destroy you in the Spirit. The battle is the Lord's, and guess what, devil: *He will give you into our hands!"*

The devil has only one purpose for you: to destroy you. He'll try to do it any way he can. And any territory you give up to him, he'll gladly take over. Never forget that.

There's a battle to be won. And once we have on the armor of God, we're ready to go out and win that battle. But we must remember when we're faced with trouble that the root of our battle is spiritual, so our armor must be spiritual.

Too often the only weapons Christians use to defeat their troubles are man-made systems. The spirit of poverty might be gripping their lives and they may face financial ruin, but they never think to put on the armor of God and to fight the battle in the spiritual realm first. No, they turn to a bank loan first as a man-made solution. Or the spirit of despair might be causing them to fall deeper and deeper into the bondage of desperation and fear, but they never think to put on the armor of God and to fight the battle in the spiritual realm first.

The Bible says we're to take up our spiritual weapons to tear down strongholds. We're to take the offensive where the works of the devil are concerned and to come against them, running at full speed toward them with our faith in motion and the word of our testimony being shouted from our hearts. As it was for David, something inside us has to rise up so that we don't back down from the devil when he taunts us.

The Power of Your Word of Testimony

Revelation 12:11 tells us that "they overcame him [the devil] by the blood of the Lamb and *by the word of their testimony*" (italics added). The word of your testimony is your battle cry. What is your testimony today?

What is your word, your confession, your declaration about who God is to you and about what God will do in your situation? What are you saying to the devil in the midst of your struggle?

Your spoken word has great power. That's not wishful

thinking. That's Bible thinking. That's not something human beings made up to suit themselves. That's something God established.

In Genesis 1 we read that God did two things in the beginning. He moved and He spoke. Notice verse 3 of that chapter: "And God *said*, 'Let there be light,' and there was light." Again and again we read in that chapter, "And God *said*...."

How did God create? He spoke. How did God change all that was without form, void and dark into something that had form, meaning, substance, energy, light, purpose and beauty? He spoke.

In that first chapter of Genesis we also read that God created humanity "in his own image...male and female He created them" (Gen. 1:27).

How does God expect you, who are in His image, to create something good out of something bad? By your speaking God's words. How does God expect you to change something that is void and formless and dark into something that is meaningful and whole and alive? By your speaking God's words!

In Hebrews 11, verses 1 and 3, we read, "Now faith is the substance of things hoped for, the evidence of things not seen....For by faith we understand that the worlds were framed *by the word of God*." God exercised His faith in His own word to give visible reality to those things which He already knew would be—and they were created.

We are to operate with that same faith level, assured that what we believe is of God *will* be made manifest on the earth when we speak out of our faith the word of God. Jesus talked about this very thing, as recorded in Mark 11:23-24. He said, "For assuredly I say to you, whoever *says* to this mountain, 'Be removed and be cast into the sea,' and does not doubt in his heart, but believes that those things he *says* will come to pass, he will have whatever he *says*. Therefore I say to you, whatever things you *ask*

135

when you pray, believe that you receive them, and you will have them." Notice the number of times the word "say" or "ask" appears in that passage.

Do you believe that when God said, "Let there be light," God fully expected there to be light? I believe that God looked within His own heart and mind and saw the world, the firmament, the heavens with its stars and sun and moon, the land, the fishes, the birds and all the animals. He knew without doubt that it would come to be just as He envisioned it when He spoke the words.

Why do I believe that? Because after God had spoken all of creation into existence, He said, "It's good." In other words, "It's just as wonderful as I thought it would be." It wasn't a surprise to God that creation was beautiful, that it worked perfectly and that it had purpose and meaning. It was what He had in mind. It was as good as He knew it would be all along.

In so creating the world, God set up a precedent for creating that applies to you and me today. There's power in your words when they're coupled with your faith. There's power you haven't even begun to know or use.

The devil knows about that power. That's why he does everything in his power to get you to speak his words and to give voice to his doubts and tales of gloom, despair and destruction. He's a liar and he wants you to repeat his lies.

The devil comes at you constantly saying many things to you about your own life. He tells you things about yourself, your family, your future and those around you. It's a steady stream of lies. And if you don't have on the helmet of salvation every day and aren't fully aware of the devil's strategy, those lies can take root in your mind. Soon you're repeating those lies: I'm just a failure. I'm a nobody. I'm poor. I'm sick. I'm stupid. I'm a rotten louse. I'm unfit for human consumption. I'm a disaster area.

Guess who's the primary audience listening to those lies about yourself? You are, of course. Your ears pick up what your mouth is saying and it takes them in, so that the problem becomes a cycle. Out of your mouth, into your ear, into your mind, out of your mouth—and so on.

Soon you believe you are all those bad things you've been saying you are. You believe what you say and you say what you believe. You live out the devil's lie until the devil has you just where he wants you—up in the hills of your life, cowering for cover, saying, "I'm going to get killed by the Philistines. It's all over for me. I can't do this. I can't win this battle. Woe is me." And if things don't change, you'll sit there under the siege of the enemy until you do die.

Often when I ask people, "How are you doing?" they respond, "Well, I'm doing pretty well under the circumstances." So I answer, "Under the circumstances? Well, what are you doing under there?" Why sit under the circumstances that are the result of your past, believing that those circumstances will dictate your future?

Anytime the devil comes to tell me about my present or my past, I tell him about his future. I tell him that he's doomed to hell, to be bound in chains for a thousand years, and eventually cast into the bottomless pit of everlasting darkness forevermore. And then I proceed to tell him about his past, that he's the one who rebelled against God and was cast out of heaven, defeated by the blood of the cross, and that he's the one who is actually standing under my feet today, according to the Word of God.

I come running at him with truth about the situation. I refuse to sit around on the hillside of my life listening to his lies. I'm not about to sit down under my circumstances. That's a horrible place to sit down!

But to talk to the devil that way, you must start with faith. What you say to the devil must be what you first believe in your heart.

You must believe that God has ordained you to be the head and not the tail (Deut. 28:13).

You must believe that God wants to meet your needs

according to His riches in glory through Christ Jesus (Phil. 4:19).

You must believe that God has ordained you to be the righteousness of God (2 Cor. 5:21).

You must believe that you are to be more than a conqueror in all things (Rom. 8:37).

You must believe God's Word before there's any power at all in speaking it. You must believe that Jesus has already won the battle. You must believe that the victory is already pre-established in heaven, and that all you need to do is go out and fight it, because the victory is yours.

Romans 10:6-7 says, "But the righteousness of faith speaks in this way [or "faith speaks in this way"]. Do not say in your heart, 'Who shall ascend into heaven?' [that is, to bring Christ down from above] or 'Who shall descend into the abyss?' [that is, to bring up Christ again from the dead]."

Now what does that mean? I believe it means that you can't pull Jesus down out of heaven by your works. You can't pull Him up from the grave by your works. It's already happened. Jesus has already come down out of heaven and established His spiritual authority over this earth by shedding His blood and dying on the cross. Jesus has already risen from the dead and ascended back into heaven. When Jesus said on the cross, "It is finished," He meant it. It was finished. The work was done. The victory was established.

Romans 10:8 continues by telling us how faith really operates: " 'The word is near you, even in your mouth and in your heart' (that is, the word of faith which we preach)." Now watch what faith *says*. Romans 10:9 continues, "That if you *confess with your mouth* the Lord Jesus and *believe in your heart* that God has raised Him from the dead, you will be saved. For with the heart one believes to righteousness, and with the mouth confession is made to salvation" (italics added).

The word "salvation" here is equal to the word "deliverance." This isn't talking only about your born-again experience. It's talking about any time you need to be "saved" or "delivered" from the clutches of evil. The same principle that brought you initial spiritual birth works throughout your Christian experience. The pattern is established right in these verses:

First, you believe in your heart what the Word of God says about a situation.

Second, with your mouth you speak out a "confession" or a declaration of what you believe.

With this, the rubber meets the road, and the reality of what you believe is released into your life.

Look at Deuteronomy 30. This portion of Scripture is one of the best-kept secrets in the Bible. In it God says plainly to His people—all His people, including you and me today as His children—that if they will obey the voice of the Lord and His commandments, He will make them prosperous in all their work, that their children will turn out right, and that the Lord will be pleased with them (or in other words, they will know and feel the approval of God).

Then God says that the ability to make this happen is "not too mysterious for you, nor is it far off. It is not in heaven, that you should say, 'Who will ascend into heaven for us and bring it to us, that we may hear it and do it?' Nor is it beyond the sea, that you should say, 'Who will go over the sea for us and bring it to us, that we may hear it and do it?' But the word is very near you, *in your mouth and in your heart*, that you may do it" (Deut. 30:11-14).

What is it that they have the ability to determine by what is in their mouths and in their hearts? Life and good, or death and evil (Deut. 30:15). A few verses later in that same chapter God says to His people, "I have set before you life and death, blessing and cursing: therefore choose life."

Choose life! Believe for life. Believe for blessing. Believe for good. Speak out for life. Speak out for blessing. Speak out for good.

God gives His people a specific agenda here. They are to:
1. Love the Lord their God.
2. Walk in His ways.
3. Keep His commandments, His judgments and His statutes.
And what will God do?
1. Cause them to live.
2. Cause them to multiply.
3. Cause them to be blessed.
4. Cause them to possess the land.

This is God's plan for you today, just as it was His plan in the past for those who loved Him, kept His commandments and chose to walk in His ways. God's plan is for you to live, multiply, be blessed and possess the land.

Are you aware that God has a land for you to possess? It's His plan for you to possess certain things in your spirit, mind, body, finances, family life, church, work—every area of your life. He wants you to possess good health. He wants you to possess the amount of money and the things you need to live, to do your work for Him and to multiply your witness for the gospel's sake. He wants you to possess good relationships with your family, coworkers, fellow church members and friends.

It's truly a matter of life and death. Goliath is standing nearby, shouting out, "If I win, you'll be our slaves. But if you win, we'll be your slaves." There's no middle-ground for compromise. It's one way toward life, multiplication and blessing, or the other way toward death, defeat and despair. It's make-it or break-it time. And God says you have the ability to determine which way things will go by what you hold in your heart and by what you say in your mouth.

You have the ability to determine which way your life will be lived out. You decide by your will. You decide what you will hold in your heart or what you will believe. You decide what you will say with your mouth or what you will declare. God says plainly that the choice is yours. Then

He gives you a good piece of divine advice: Choose life!

We find a word of supreme caution and danger in the midst of this chapter. Deuteronomy 30:17-18 spells it out: "But if your heart turns away so that you do not hear, and are drawn away, and worship other gods and serve them... you shall surely perish."

We're right back to what we said before about the devil's lies. If you listen to the wrong voice in your spirit and hear only the devil's lies, so that you worship what he sets up before you as false idols, then you've started down the wrong path, and that path leads to your destruction. You won't just suffer—you'll perish. Die. And die eternally.

Life and blessing or death and cursing. That's the choice.

Proverbs 18:21 puts it all in a nutshell: "Death and life are in the power of the tongue, and those who love it will eat its fruit."

When you understand that, every time the devil comes at you with his shouts of defiance and his lies about your past, present and future, you hold the key to life or death by what you believe and by what you say, *then* you'll truly prize the word of your testimony. You'll start paying attention like never before to what you say and to what you hold to be true in your heart. When you really understand that what you believe and what you say hold the key to whether things move toward life and blessing or toward death and cursing, then you'll put much more value on your heart and your words. You'll watch more closely every word that you say because you'll understand that you're about to eat the fruit of that word, and it will be food for your life or food for your death.

Many people have wondered for a number of years now about how we've withstood so many tests and trials at the Church on the Rock. I'll tell you. Every time the devil has come to me with his defiant cries and lies, saying, "I'm going to knock the Church on the Rock right off the map. I'm going to crush Larry Lea. I'm going to put a stop to the ministry of prayer across this nation. I'm going to defeat the warriors of God at the Church on the Rock''—it's in that moment that I pay very close attention to the word of my testimony.

I could say one of two things. I could say, "Yes, things are bad, and they're probably going to get worse. I don't know if they're ever going to change. It's foolishness to think we could build a church thirty-five miles east of Dallas and move out from there to take Dallas for Jesus Christ, and from there, the nation. It just isn't going to work." That's what the natural man wants to say. I readily admit that's the first thought that pops into my head because that's the natural man getting in the first word.

But I've decided I won't live by the natural man. I'll live by the spiritual man. And the spiritual man is connected with the Holy Spirit man, Jesus Christ. I've made a decision in my life that the natural man will be put under the subjection of my spiritual man. So I won't say things that lead toward decline, destruction or death. It's my decision what I will believe in my heart. It's my choice, by my will, just what I will say. Those negative words of the natural man would be a "word of testimony" that bears the fruit of death and cursing. Instead I'll choose life.

I say, "No, devil, you're wrong. I am the righteousness of God and you're the one who will be defeated by the power of the Holy Spirit resident in me. The Church on the Rock will thrive. It will grow and its ministry will spread throughout the nation and around the world, defeating you and your demons from here on the plains of battle all the way to the gates of the city of heaven. We'll put your demons to flight and take the spoils of your tents. We'll win this battle, overcome this circumstance and see God change this situation. Just watch our slingshots start to whirl in your direction!"

Those are words of life. They are words based on the word of life. It's God's will that His people defeat the devil and take the kingdom of God. It's God's will that they experience peace, joy and righteousness every day they walk this earth. It's God's will that we live, multiply, are blessed and possess what God wants us to have.

The Value of a Good Report

A story in Numbers 13 reminds us of the value of a good report, as well as the destructive power of a bad report. There we read that the children of Israel had left Egypt under the leadership of Moses. They had crossed the Red Sea and were headed for Canaan, the "promised land." God told Moses to send out twelve men from the camp, one from each of the twelve tribes of Israel. They were to look over the land they were about to enter, and spy it out.

Now they weren't sent out in order to determine whether or not they could take the land. They weren't ordered to come back prepared to vote whether or not they could defeat the enemy. No, they were sent out to see how the battle should be fought and how good the victory would be. They were told to bring back some of the fruit of the land to encourage the people that it was indeed a land "flowing with milk and honey" as God had promised. And they were told to get a good line on where and how the people lived, how they were armed and what the cities were like. They were a reconnaissance team, sent out to get information so that when they got back, the generals could get together and map out a strategy before God.

What happened? Ten of the twelve men came back terrified. They returned with more than information. They came back with an opinion, a *belief*. And their belief was that there was no way the children of Israel could win the land. Only Joshua and Caleb came back with a good report.

What did the other ten have to say? They reported: "The land, through which we have gone as spies, is a land that devours its inhabitants, and all the people whom we saw in it are men of great stature. There we saw the giants (the descendants of Anak came from the giants); and we were like grasshoppers in our own sight, and so we were in their sight" (Num. 13:32-33).

Now this was the opposite of what God had told them. God had said, "I will give you a land flowing with milk and honey"—which means a good, fertile and prosperous land. God had said, "You'll be able to take the land. It's yours. Don't worry about it. Just hear and obey, and you'll win this thing. Walk in My Spirit and you can't lose."

But the ten spies forgot the word of God. Instead they focused their attention on the circumstances, the problems, the people that looked like giants, the size of their cities, the armies and their weapons. They came to an opinion that what God had said wasn't true.

The Bible calls their report a "bad report." What makes a report bad? It's a report that's contrary to what God has already said about the situation. God had said "life" and "blessing" to them about the land of Canaan. They were saying "death" and "cursing." It was 180 degrees opposite to God's word about the situation. And that made it a "bad report."

But what about the report of Joshua and Caleb? Here is the word of their testimony: "The land we passed through to spy out is an exceedingly good land. If the Lord delights in us, then He will bring us into this land and give it to us, 'a land which flows with milk and honey.' Only rebel not ye against the Lord, neither fear ye the people of the land; for they are bread for us: their defence is departed from them, and the Lord is with us: fear them not" (Num. 14:7-9, KJV).

In other words, they were saying, "God said we can go over and take the land. God said it's ours. God said He doesn't intend for us to wander in this wilderness. God said He wants us to have the land of Canaan as our 'promised land.' So let's go!" They had the right idea.

But the people heard the ten instead of the two. They bought the bad report. The Bible says they "lifted up their voice and cried and wept that night" and that they took up stones as if to stone Joshua and Caleb to death. The result was death and a curse for all those who refused to believe and speak the word of God.

Every one of them, except Joshua and Caleb, died in the wilderness and never saw the land of Canaan. Their children got to go into the promised land, but none of those who disbelieved and who repeated the negative report were allowed to live to see the victory.

What is in the power of your believing and speaking? Life and blessing or death and cursing. Where is your ability to exercise your faith? It's very near you. How near? It's as near as your mouth. It's as near as what you believe in your heart.

I'm Not Talking About Idle Confession

I can just hear some of you say, "But I don't believe all this name-it-and-claim-it theology I hear." I'm not talking about some kind of aimless "name-it-claim-it" idea. I'm not talking about anything that is rooted in greed or selfish ambition. I'm not talking about "speaking out" things that aren't in the Word of God.

I'm talking about believing the Word of God about a situation and then speaking the Word of God in that situation. How do you get to the place where you know with a certainty that you are believing the right things? Look at the first three verses of Psalm 1:

> Blessed is the man
> Who walks not in the counsel of the ungodly,
> Nor stands in the path of sinners,
> Nor sits in the seat of the scornful;
> But his delight is in the law of the Lord,
> And in His law he meditates day and night.

He shall be like a tree
Planted by the rivers of water,
That brings forth its fruit in its season,
Whose leaf also shall not wither;
And whatever he does shall prosper.

The key to believing the right things is "meditating on God's law day and night." Now "meditating" here does not refer to some Eastern form of mysticism. It literally means "to ponder by talking to yourself." It means voicing the laws of God over and over to yourself, letting their meaning sink in and soak in. It means "hearing with your ears" and letting faith rise up within you. It means memorizing God's laws and precepts and setting your mind to dwell on them.

What happens to those who do this? The psalmist tells us that they have deep roots. They aren't easily blown over by the winds of change or the storms of life.

They bring forth fruit. They not only *know* God's laws, but they also *do* God's laws.

They are "evergreen." They aren't what I call "withering saints"—worn down by life. They don't fade in and out of their Christian walk. They persevere. They are constant in their pursuit of God's desires. They are determined to live out God's plan for their lives.

They are prosperous. They see "multiplication" of the good things in their lives.

And finally, out of that daily meditation on the things of God, continually pondering them by talking them out, they come to a deep knowing of God's plan. They see it as a whole. They feel God's heartbeat. They hear God's voice. And when they're hearing God's voice and taking His words into their lives and building their lives around them, then when the time comes to speak to the devil, they're just repeating what they've already heard from God. They're just passing along His absolute truth.

That kind of meditation on God's word brings us back to the blood of Jesus. When you're faced with a situation or circumstance that spells trouble in your life, ask yourself, What did the blood of the Lamb purchase for me in this situation?

I'll tell you what the blood of the Lamb did *not* purchase for you. It did *not* purchase:

- guilt or condemnation;
- exasperation or frustration;
- greed or selfish ambition;
- depression;
- fear.

No, the blood of Jesus purchased life for your soul and for your body. It broke the power of sin and sickness over you. There may be many things you don't know about the will of God concerning a situation, but you can be assured of many things concerning the blood of Jesus Christ. You can be assured that His blood purchased for you deliverance and salvation from the enemy.

But, you may say, what about the things outside of my control? What about my environment and my genetic makeup?

Yes, it's true that you've inherited certain environmental and genetic realities. I'm not denying that you were given a certain "starting point" in your life. But that doesn't need to be your "ending point."

Today, in the spiritual realm, "environmentally" you are seated with Christ in heavenly places (Eph. 2:6). That's your new environment. Today, in the spiritual realm, "genetically" you are washed in the blood of the Lamb (Rev. 7:14); you are a child of God and a joint heir with Jesus Christ of His riches in glory (1 John 3:1; Rom. 8:17).

In getting from where you are in the natural to where you are in the spiritual, you can believe that God is turning things around. He's redesigning you and causing new things to happen within you so that the more you press into God and keep your heart believing Him and your mouth speaking a good word of testimony, God will create in you His glory. You are growing from grace to grace and moving from glory to glory in Christ Jesus.

Have you ever heard someone say, "Well, my dad was an alcoholic and his dad was an alcoholic, and I just know I'll be an alcoholic"? Or "Well, I just have a manic personality"? Or maybe "I just have addictive tendencies"?

If you've ever said that in your own life, let the blood of Jesus Christ cover that tendency. Say, "You're right, devil, I'll drink; but I'll drink of the 'new wine' of the Holy Spirit and the fountain of eternal life." Say, "I'll get manic about the Word of God. The dictionary says that manic people express an 'excessive enthusiasm or passion,' so that's what I'll have about the Word of God!" Say, "I'll be addicted all right—to the ministry of the saints, to serving God and His people, to reading my Bible and praying daily, to fellowshipping with God's people."

Life or death is in the word of your testimony. Blessing or cursing. It's up to you.

Have you ever gone through a season of depression? I'm not talking about when you got up one morning and even after two or three cups of coffee you felt a little down. I'm talking about when you were lower than a snake's belly

What happens? The devil comes around with one of his first-class lies, saying, "You're just a depressive personality. You'll always suffer with this. It's in your genetic code · to be this way."

Depression is like a punishment. Are you aware of that? Those who suffer depression have the same feeling that a child has right after being severely punished. They feel useless, rejected and unwanted, and their first desire is to crawl into a hole and pull it over their heads.

I know because I've experienced some of that in my past. But do you know what I say when depression tries to crawl back into my life? I say, "Listen up, devil! The Bible says that Jesus bore the chastisement of my peace. He bore the punishment feeling that robs me of my peace of heart and mind. So I don't have to experience this. I won't take it from you. I'll have the joy, peace and righteousness of God in my life because that's what God's Word says. I'm making God's Word the word of my testimony!''

My grandfather died of a heart attack when he was sixty-four years old and my uncle has heart disease, so my father started fearing some time ago that he would die in the next few years. I said to him, "Daddy, stand on your feet and say in the name of Jesus, 'By Jesus' stripes I am healed, and I'll live until it's time for God to take me out of my body so that I can be with Him and without any limitations!' ''

You may think I'm denying reality. No, I'm denying the power of past and present circumstances to govern or dictate the future of my life. I'm believing the true reality of who I am in Jesus Christ and what God has promised to me in His Word. I'm choosing life. I'm choosing blessing. I'm choosing to walk in His commandments and according to His Spirit, and to live out every day of my life in the joy, peace and righteousness God wants me to have as my blessing.

If you're in business, has the devil ever come to you and said, "Well, your business is doing OK today but this good time will blow over"? If you're a pastor, has the devil ever come to you with that same lie about your church?

He's come to me with that line. And he's even used a fellow minister to deliver it. He said, "Now, Larry, I'll tell you what will happen. The 'new' has worn off you and people are fickle. The Church on the Rock and other independent charismatic churches like it are just one of those phenomena that will blow over after awhile."

How did I respond? I said: "Yes, it will blow over all right. The Spirit of God will blow over Rockwall. Then He'll blow over Mesquite, Garland and North Dallas. Pretty soon He'll blow over all of Dallas and Fort Worth. Then just watch Him blow over this nation!''

What about your money? What lie is the devil feeding you on that topic? Have you ever walked down the aisle at the grocery mart when suddenly you notice how the prices have gone up? And the devil whispers in your ear, ''You won't have enough money to buy groceries *and* to give your tithe at church on Sunday morning.''

That's one of his favorite temptations, and it's one of the most effective. Because when God's people stop giving to God's work, then God's work isn't extended. No ''enemy territory'' is threatened by God's people. No message of conviction goes out to touch the hearts of the lost. No healing work enters areas of desperate need. When the money dries up, the things that money buys—whether its airtime for Christian media or medicines for the missionary clinics or food and clothing for the poor or utility bills for the church—cease to be. And ultimately the preaching and doing of the gospel are stopped. All on account of money.

Melva Jo and I have experienced that very temptation. Sometime ago the Lord deeply impressed me that we were no longer to accept a salary from the church I pastor, and at the same time, we were to begin to double-tithe to the church. That's no income from the church and 20 percent to the church from other sources. Now why did I do that? Not because it looked like a smart thing to do from my mind's standpoint, believe me. I did it because God told me to do it.

He said, ''Do it, and watch what I'll do.''

Now I had lots of reasons not to obey. I could easily have gone to Melva Jo in my natural-man state and said, ''God said to do this, Melva Jo, but we just can't do it now. We've got to use all our sense right now. We just got a new house with your momma and daddy out there living with us, and my nephew has just come to live with us, and goodness, that's a lot of expense, and I've got a car payment to make and—and—and—and....''

All the time a little voice of accusation was whispering in my ear, "You won't make it if you do that. You won't make it if you stop taking a salary and start double-tithing."

So what did I do? I doused all those ideas of the natural man and all those accusations of the devil—who is, as you will recall, termed the "accuser of the brethren" in Revelation 12:11—with a heavy outpouring of the blood of Jesus.

I said, "Christ has redeemed me from the curse of the law, including the curse of the human law of economics. I'm sowing my seed of faith week by week. God is my provider. He is Jehovah-jireh in my life. My tithe and offering will go in every week. I'm making a faith-dcsirc commitment to follow God's leading in my life. I'm walking in the Spirit and doing His commandments as He has directed me as a result of my reading His Word and hearing His voice, and I'm expecting the glory of God to be shown in my life. I'm believing that God will supply all of my need according to His riches in glory by Christ Jesus (Phil. 4:19). I'm believing that as I give, men will give to me pressed down, shaken together and running over according to Luke 6:38. I'm choosing blessing, not cursing. I'm choosing life, not financial death!"

And do you know what happened?

The very week after I had this showdown with the devil and began to follow what God had impressed upon my heart to do, my book *The Hearing Ear* hit the bookstands, and it eventually became a best-seller. God supplied my need, with overflow, just as He has promised. And He has continued to supply week after week, month after month.

David made a bold statement to Goliath: "The battle is the Lord's, and He will give you into our hand." What made David so certain that the battle was the Lord's?

One thing and one thing alone. David had a *knowing* that he belonged to God and God belonged to him. He knew he was of the house of Jesse, an Israelite, one of God's people. He knew his birthright.

Paul wrote to the Colossian Christians: "Christ in you, the hope of glory" (Col. 1:27). He wrote to the believers in the Galatian church: "I have been crucified with Christ; it is no longer I who live, but Christ lives in me, and the life which I now live in the flesh I live by faith in the Son of God, who loved me and gave Himself for me" (Gal. 2:20).

John wrote, "He who is in you [Christ] is greater than he [the devil] who is in the world" (1 John 4:4).

Is Christ in you today? By your belief and confession of faith, has Christ been established as king of your life? If so, then you are in Christ and Christ is in you.

For that reason, whatever the devil throws at you He is actually throwing at Christ in you. You're not really Satan's number-one enemy. Jesus Christ is Satan's number-one foe. His attempts are ultimately to wipe the name of Jesus Christ off the face of the earth. But you, as a bearer of Christ's love and power—a living witness of God's mercy and love and power—are a threat to Satan. So he comes at the Christ in you.

As David was running toward Goliath with his powerful word of testimony and his slingshot whirling, he was also casting himself fully upon God. He was saying, "God, I'm Yours. God, You are my God." David was going all the way back to God's promise to the Israelites in the time of Moses, when God had said, "You will be My people—a peculiar treasure to me among all nations—and I will be your God."

David believed the Word of God. He believed it to be true for his own life. God was his God. He was God's man. So Goliath's challenge wasn't just the dare of one soldier to another. It was the challenge of an evil man defying the host of God's people. It was a spiritual matter between those who embodied the spirit of the destroyer, the accuser, the devil himself, and those who were of God.

The taunting cries of Goliath were a challenge to God's

people, and David knew that. He said again and again to those clusters of men on the hillside, "Is not this a cause worthy of a fight?" God's reputation was being put on the line. Who would fight for it?

When sickness strikes your body, your first thought should be: This is the devil's attempt to destroy my life and therefore to diminish the body of Christ by one person; to put a stop to the work God has called me to do to extend His kingdom; to cause the testimony of God to be tarnished; to cause sadness within my family and church. So I'm casting all of my life on Jesus and claiming all of His life in me. This battle is the Lord's because I am the Lord's.

When severe financial setbacks strike your business, your first thought should be: This is the devil's attempt to put me under and therefore to stop the flow of money I can put into God's work—which will keep the gospel from being preached to those who need to hear it, and be a blight upon my witness for God and upon my church. I'm casting my entire business on Jesus and claiming all of His life in this situation. This battle is the Lord's because I am the Lord's, and this fruit of my labor belongs solely to Him.

Of course, I'm not saying that you should stop working. Haggai 2:4 spells it out: "Be strong...and work!" Nor am I saying that you're not to use every resource God has provided to battle your circumstances. If you're sick, you need a physician, you need people who will pray the prayer of faith and surround you with love and encouragement, and you need a restful environment. You need to take advantage of everything God has provided for your health.

The point is that the origin of this battle—the person who is picking the fight—is in the spiritual realm. So it's one battle in the ongoing war between Satan and his demons and God and His angels. It's up to you, by what you hold in your heart and what you speak from your mouth, to cast the deciding vote. Life or death, blessing or cursing; you decide.

What is your Goliath today? What problem is calling to you from the valley of your life? And what is your battle cry in response? What is the word of your testimony?

Let it be a strong one for the Lord. Shout it loudly and clearly today. The time has come to engage in combat.

Close the Door on the Devil Today

1) What are the biggest battles you're facing today? Write them out in a list.

2) Place your hand over that list and declare aloud: "The battle is the Lord's. I give it to Him right now!"

3) Now write out what you believe to be God's desire for you in the battles you've been facing.

4) Place your hand on these statements and declare aloud, "I believe *this* is what God has for me. I will trust Him for it!"

5) Why not write your name in the space below as a lasting reminder of your commitment to trust God for total victory in every area of your life?

_____

(Your name here)
Champion Giant-Killer in Christ Jesus

Let's pray and agree together you'll never forget that the battles you face belong to the Lord: "In the name of Jesus, I agree with you that this word is sealed forever in my heart. I declare today that the battle is Yours, Father almighty. I turn it fully over to You. I trust You with my whole life, including these situations. I cast myself totally on You. I choose life today. I choose blessing today. I choose to trust You and believe You for all You want to give to me. I look for victory to come! Amen."

NINE

Combat:
Binding the Strongman

Jesus was controversial. Not just a little. Not just occasionally. He was thoroughly, persistently controversial throughout most of His ministry.

Folks today who think they will follow Jesus, say the things He said, and do the things He did without encountering opposition are in for a rude awakening. Jesus was controversial in His day, and we who express His life and His teachings will be controversial today as well. Jesus even said so. He said to His apostles, "If they treat the master of the house as if he's the devil, how do you think they'll treat you?" (See John 13:16.)

Despite great miracles and teachings that stirred and convicted the crowds, Jesus was accused of:

- not paying His taxes.
- tricking and manipulating the people and using magic to work His miracles.
- being an illegitimate son.
- being a fraud, a liar and a cheat.
- casting out demons by the power of Beelzebub, the chief of the devils.

In Luke 11:14-26, we read that Jesus cast out a devil from a man who was unable to speak. As soon as the demon was gone, the dumb man spoke and the people marvelled. But a few scoffed, "He is casting out devils by the name of the ruler of devils."

The Bible says that Jesus knew their thoughts and responded to the critics: "Every kingdom divided against itself is brought to desolation, and a house divided against a house falls. If Satan also is divided against himself, how will his kingdom stand?...But if I cast out demons with the finger of God, surely the kingdom of God has come upon you" (Luke 11:17-20).

Jesus went on to give them this illustration: "When a strong man, fully armed, guards his own palace, his goods are in peace. But when a stronger than he comes upon him and overcomes him, he takes from him all his armor in which he trusted, and divides his spoils. He who is not with Me is against Me, and he who does not gather with Me scatters" (Luke 11:21-23).

Jesus was speaking directly about the devil and the power of his demons. He elaborated His point: "When an unclean spirit goes out of a man, he goes through dry places, seeking rest; and finding none, he says, 'I will return to my house from which I came.' And when he comes, he finds it swept and put in order. Then he goes and takes with him seven other spirits more wicked than himself, and they enter, and dwell there, and the last state of that man is worse than the first" (Luke 11:24-26).

Today God is raising up a company of people who know what the score really is, where the action really is in God. They're aware that unclean spirits are roaming this earth, seeking places to dwell in order to destroy men and women. This emerging company will have listening ears for what the Holy Spirit is saying to the church today, and they'll answer His call to battle. They know that this battle is a battle in the spirit realm, and they are ready for combat.

The Bible teaches that "though we walk in the flesh, we

do not war according to the flesh...the weapons of our warfare are not carnal, but mighty in God for the pulling down of strongholds, casting down arguments and every high thing that exalts itself against the knowledge of God, bringing every thought into captivity to the obedience of Christ" (2 Cor. 10:3-5).

In another place the apostle Paul calls this great struggle a wrestling match, but he makes it clear that we do not "wrestle against flesh and blood, but against principalities, against powers, against the rulers of the darkness of this age, against spiritual hosts of wickedness in high places" (Eph. 6:12).

A war is going on for our nation today. A war is being fought for our metropolitan areas, our great cities across this land. There's a war raging for our churches, for our families, and for each of us personally.

It's a war in the spirit realm, and this is the challenge you face: The devil has sent messengers, strong principalities and powers, to stand against you and to keep you from being and doing all that God has called you to be and do. *So what will you do about it?*

More specifically, how will you bind the strongman coming against your life—the one who comes to steal, kill and destroy God's eternal purposes in your life? How will you fight him and win?

God has provided for us an effective way to fight a good fight of faith and to overcome those powers. But if you don't learn how to fight that fight, you'll be overcome. We're talking about hand-to-hand combat!

Some of you have been attacked in your bodies, and you need to learn how to beat off the spirits of infirmity. Some of you have been attacked in your finances, and you need to learn how to whip those spirits of poverty that are coming against your money. Some of you have been attacked in your marriages, and you need to learn how to defeat those spirits of hatred and lust that are trying to destroy the love in your marriage.

God knows exactly what is coming against you. He knows exactly where you stand. And He's ready to work on your behalf if you will only fight. So let's learn how to stand, how to fight, how to pull down those strongholds, and how to win!

Recently as I was flying into a major city in this nation, we began to descend through a smoggy cloud toward the airport. We could see the sun above, but as we descended into the cloud we couldn't see the ground below. While I was praying in the spirit during those final few minutes of our flight, I had a spiritual vision that paralleled my physical look at this city. In my spirit I saw a dark cloud over that city.

I said, "Lord, what is that cloud?"

He spoke in my spirit, "That is the strongman and his minions hovering." Then He showed me that similar clouds of darkness were over every major city in our nation.

I cried out in my spirit, "What shall we do? That cloud must be removed!"

The Lord answered, "Son, that's what the three hundred thousand intercessors in America are all about."

God called me several years ago to raise up three hundred thousand men and women who would pray daily and intercede for America. That's the heartbeat of my ministry as I go from city to city across this nation. And when the Lord spoke that into my spirit, I immediately had a vision of those three hundred thousand intercessors lifting up their hands to God.

As they lifted up their hands, they were poking holes in the cloud of darkness with their fingertips. I was reminded again of that verse of Scripture in Luke: "*But if I cast out demons with the finger of God*, surely the kingdom of God has come upon you" (Luke 11:20, italics added). As those intercessors raised their hands, and their fingers poked holes through the clouds of darkness, the sunlight and the glory of God streamed through.

Your hands today are the extended hands of Jesus. Your hands are the only hands He has today in this world. When you lift up your hands into the air and declare with your mouth that the North, South, East and West must give up what belongs to God, you dislodge the strongman from his place over us.

The sun doesn't know how to do anything but shine. It never turns off, though it's sometimes covered from our view by clouds. The same is true for the Son of God. He never stops shining, but His glory is sometimes hidden from our view by dark spiritual clouds. When the powers of darkness are forced to flee and the strongman is bound, then the kingdom of God shines through and the glory of the Lord is manifested on the earth.

What is the nature of this spiritual cloud that may over-shadow a city? It's a spirit of darkness that obscures the glory of God and covers up the kingdom of God with sin and strife.

Over many cities a spirit of religion reigns. That's the spirit that divides brother from brother and says, "I'm a Baptist"—or some other denomination—"and you're a Methodist so there's no fellowship between us." Or "I'm a charismatic and you're a Catholic so there's no love flow-ing between us." Whatever denominations may be in-volved, this spirit insists on dividing the church. With the spirit of religion, dogma is more important than Jesus. But when we resist this spirit, we must insist that everyone who names the name of Jesus Christ and holds that name as their only hope for salvation is our brother or sister.

Over some cities are spirits of avarice and greed. Over others are spirits of violence. Over still others are spirits of addiction. So the only thing that will change what is go-ing on in our cities is an army of intercessors who will stand and raise their hands in prayer and praise to poke holes in the darkness.

When enough holes are poked in the darkness, what happens? The cloud collapses. It evaporates. It ceases to be. Sunshine explodes over the face of the earth. We sing it in our song of praise: "Arise, shine, for the glory of the Lord is come!"

Do you recall what happened on the day of Pentecost? The people were gathered together in prayer. They were coming together in "one accord," in one spirit, in one attitude of prayer before God. They weren't studying. They weren't sermonizing. They weren't memorizing Bible verses or spiritual slogans. They were *praying*. And when the glory of God broke through on that crowd, signs and wonders and salvations followed.

Peter only needed to stand up and say, "This is what was promised. Let me tell you about Jesus..." and three thousand people were saved through one sermon. (See Acts 2 and 3.) Not three thousand sermons to save one soul, which is the way it seems to happen most often today. No—one sermon was enough for three thousand souls.

A number of years ago, shortly after I was converted and began to preach, my friend Jerry and I conducted a revival in Prospect, Texas, a little town just a few miles north of Rockwall. In those days Jerry preached and I led the singing. When we entered a town, we would usually meet together after the first service to ask God to show us the enemy forces at work in that particular town or church. Then we'd come against those spirits and bind them.

We had only been saved and filled with the Holy Spirit a year or so, but we knew it was God's will that His light and power would come upon the people. We believed with all our hearts what I still believe today: It is not God's will that any should perish, but that all should come to know the Lord. (See 2 Pet. 3:9.) We felt strongly that it was our responsibility as evangelists to tear apart the spiritual darkness so that God's light could shine with full force on the people who heard us preach and sing and testify of His greatness.

As Jerry and I were praying on Saturday of that particular revival week, the Lord revealed to us that a spirit of fear dominated that church. He showed us especially the great fear in the pastor's heart. We got down in a little back room of that church and began to bind the spirit of fear. We declared that a spirit of boldness and courage would come over the people and be released in that area.

Now in many Baptist church revivals the custom is for the evangelist and the pastor to go "witnessing" in the afternoons and then to conduct services in the evening. On that Saturday I said to the pastor, "Let's go witness to the roughest sinner in town."

So he said, "OK. Let's go see ol' Harold Bull." Even his name sounded tough to me!

We drove over to Harold's house, and Jerry stayed in the car to pray as the pastor and I went to the door. Harold had just come from his tractor. He was probably only about six feet, four inches tall but he *looked* at least seven feet tall to me as he stood there behind the screen door of his house. He was dirty and he had a mean look on his face. The chaw of tobacco in his mouth looked about the size of a baseball.

The pastor started to speak, but when he opened his mouth, his voice cracked. In a voice three notes too high he finally stammered out, "Hello, Harold, we've come to talk to you about our revival meeting."

Harold just stared him down. Never said a word. Just stared.

Now I had prayed with Jerry for about four hours that morning, so I was dangerous at that particular moment. I was so full of God I was ready to spit holy nails. Suddenly I heard myself saying, "Harold, what we really came out here to say is this: Do you want to be saved?"

Harold nearly swallowed that tobacco. He turned to stare at me. I got him in an eye-to-eye look. In my mind's eye,

161

I could imagine him tearing through that screen door and ripping my little head right off my body. But in my physical eyes, I looked at him with the love of Jesus and I didn't back down. I didn't have any fear in my heart. I just kept looking at him.

Finally he said, "Yeah, I want to be saved."

I said, "Then get out here on the front porch, Harold." He came out from behind the door and stood on the porch with us. I said, "Now bow your head and spit out that tobacco and be reverent because we're going to pray."

He spit out his tobacco and bowed his head, and we prayed. And ol' Harold got saved that afternoon!

Then I said, "Now, Harold, if you really mean this, you'll come to church, you'll walk down the aisle of that church and you'll make a public confession of your faith before God and everyone."

We had revival that night and a few folks got saved, but Harold wasn't there. On Sunday morning, we started the song service and Harold wasn't there. We sang one song, and then another, and then another—and still no Harold.

Then suddenly the back door opened in that little wooden church, and there stood Harold. He nearly filled the door frame, and as he walked forward, you could hear his big work boots on the wooden floor. It was suddenly as if we were filming an E.F. Hutton commercial. When Harold walked in and sat down, everyone's head turned, and the place got so quiet you could have heard a pin drop.

Harold sat down, and Jerry stood up to preach. When Jerry gave the invitation to come forward and accept Jesus Christ, Harold stood up, walked forward and publicly gave his heart to Jesus.

Word spread like wildfire through that town that ol' Harold Bull had gone forward and been saved. By that night the little church was packed out. People were standing along the side walls of the church because there were no more chairs and no more room in the pews.

That night Jerry and I decided to lay hands on the people, every one of them. We didn't know any better than to do that in a Baptist church. We had been to a meeting where the minister walked around and laid hands on the people and prayed for them, so we decided we'd do that, too. And let me tell you, that place came *alive* that night!

Now I am 100-percent convinced that our revival services would have never been successful in that town and in that church unless Jerry and I had first prayed and discerned the nature of the strongman over the church and the town and then prayed that God would defeat the strongman and release His kingdom. I don't believe Harold would have been saved or the lives of that community changed on that Sunday morning without intercessory prayer first pushing holes through the darkness that had bound that church in fear.

What will you do when you're hit by the devil? Will you back up and back down? Or will you stay in there and fight with all your might?

What will you do when you see darkness over a place—a city, a church, a family or even yourself? Will you turn and run? Or will you get into intercessory prayer, discern the nature of that strongman and then bind him in the name of Jesus to poke your holes through that cloud of darkness?

God is raising up people today who are willing to say, "Hit me once, hit me twice, hit me as many times as you think you can—but I'm standing my ground. I'll get right back up and be here in the morning, same time, same channel. I'll be standing here, getting stronger and stronger with every blow." That's the spirit of God's warriors! That's the spirit of those who will wrestle and win, not against flesh and blood, but against principalities, powers, rulers of darkness and spiritual wickedness.

How do you stand your ground?

1. Name the thing that is lording it over you, and declare that Jesus will be Lord in its place.

Are you facing a battle with doubt? You know it's doubt because you're spending your time wondering about this and that, questioning whether Jesus is your Savior, questioning whether you are born again or if you can ever be born again. Name it for what it is. And then declare out loud, "Doubt, you will not be my lord. Jesus is my Lord!"

Are you facing a battle with lust? You know it's lust because you spend all your time imagining relationships with people you see, hear or read about. Men, you know that's what it is when your head nearly swivels off your neck everytime a pretty girl walks by. Declare out loud, "Lust, you will not be my lord. Jesus is my Lord!"

Are you facing a battle with fear? You're scared all the time, and even though you know in your mind that you may not have any reason for your fear, you're still afraid? Are you looking under your bed and behind every bush, expecting trouble? Declare, "Fear, you will not be my lord. Jesus is my Lord!"

Are you facing a battle with loneliness? You feel alone even in a crowd of people? You feel apart and behind a wall even when you're having a conversation with a dear friend? Declare today, "Loneliness, you will not be my lord. Jesus is my Lord!"

Are you facing a battle with greed? You want things just for the sake of having them, not because you need them, but because they're there and you don't have them? You can't get away from it. It haunts you day and night. So declare out loud right now, "Greed, you will not be my lord. Jesus is my Lord!"

No matter what it is you're facing today, you can be assured of one thing: You're not the first person or the only person facing this battle. These spirits are commonly faced by everyone at some time or another. No one is immune from their harassment.

You're at a point of testing, of going through a fire, of facing a battle. The devil, God and you will all see what you're made of by the way you respond. And you can respond the right way by standing up to the spirit that's bringing bondage into your life. You can say, "You won't lord it over me! Jesus is my Lord!"

It's in your power and your authority to stand up and declare that the spiritual powers of darkness will not have lordship over your life. They will not rule you. They will not govern your behavior. They will not capture your thought life. They will not lead you into temptation and sin.

It's in your power and your authority as a believer in Jesus Christ, bought and paid for and washed clean by His blood, to stand and say, "Jesus is Lord."

When I was in seminary, I felt so alone at times, so dry in my spirit, so lost. I was studying Greek, Hebrew, philosophy, hermeneutics and homiletics—dry old subjects—all in one semester. And I said, "Dear Lord, I didn't know there was so much to learn about the kingdom of God." My mind was going this way and that, and my spirit had a bad case of the "dries." I was starting to become angry and bitter, and I could just see myself becoming a mean little ol' preacher.

But I made a determination right then and there. I prayed, "Lord, I won't let the 'dries' be the lord of my life. Jesus, You will be the Lord of my life." Day after day I prayed that to the Lord. I declared it to be so in my life. And do you know what happened? I came alive in my spirit. I had joy. I felt the fellowship of believers around me.

The same thing can happen to you—if you wake up from your spiritual sleep pattern. No more drowsing! No more being lulled by the spirits of slumber in your inner man. It's time to wake up and face the battle.

How can you tell whether a particular spirit is truly a "strongman" in your life? Everyone, of course, has natural tendencies and natural temptations. That's not what I'm talking about here. Many temptations and tendencies can be dealt with by your recognizing them, repenting of them, turning to God, and then moving forward in your life.

These forces of greed, lust, fear, loneliness, doubt and other problems become "strongmen" in your life when they reach the point where they confront you constantly. They drive you, they overwhelm you, they attempt to overtake you—and they never let up. That thing that eats away at you all the time; that thought that comes again and again and again; that desire so overpowering that you don't know what to do about it—that is a strongman. It's a spirit that has attached itself to your being in a strong way. It has a stronghold on your life and it won't let go.

Remember: A strongman never comes to show you a good time. It comes to hinder your life, and eventually to kill you. It comes to take away your self-esteem, your future and your family.

My dad didn't have any trouble identifying the strongman that held him in bondage. He said to me one day, "You know, some men can drink a beer and they never even think about it after that. But I drink one beer and I break out in spots."

I said, "What do you mean, you break out in spots?"

He said, "I break out in spots: in Los Angeles, in New York, in New Orleans. You'll find me breaking out in spots where they serve alcohol all over this nation."

That's the mark of someone who has an addiction that marks his life. You must come to the point where you can identify that strongman for who and what it is. Behind every vice at work on this earth you'll find a principality, a power, at its root. You'll find a strongman waiting to take over the "goods"—the good things, the good traits, the good skills, the goodness—of your life.

When people yield themselves to a vice often enough, the power of that vice becomes attached to them and they soon become driven by it. They no longer merely think a thought; the thought is dictating to them. They no longer are committing that sin; that sin is defining who they are.

And it's at this point that the strongman "overcomes you and divides his spoils" (Luke 11:22).

So you must identify the strongman, and declare that Jesus will be Lord in his place.

2. You must bind that strongman with the name of Jesus and the Word of God.

To do this, you must first recognize that you have power and authority over the strongman in the name of Jesus. Proverbs 18:10 says, "The name of the Lord is a strong tower; the righteous run to it and are safe." The name of Jesus is your "strong tower"—your fortress against the enemy.

The name of Jesus is above every name. Ephesians 1:20-22 describes the authority given to Jesus by His Father, God almighty:

> Which He worked in Christ when He raised Him from the dead and seated Him at His right hand in the heavenly places, far above all principality and power and might and dominion, and every name that is named, not only in this age but also in that which is to come. And He put all things under His feet....

Now "all things" means just that. All things. Nothing—absolutely nothing—is more powerful than Jesus. And when we speak in His name on the earth, calling forth those things which Jesus wants to see accomplished on the earth, nothing can inhibit those things from coming to pass.

Notice carefully that I said we are to call forth in the name of Jesus those things which Jesus wants to see accomplished. The name of Jesus is not something we use lightly or casually to get the things we want. It releases the power of Jesus on the earth to get done what He wants done.

It's as if we've been given a signed blank check from the account of Jesus Christ of Nazareth, an account with infinite riches of all types to meet every form of human need.

167

We, as stewards of that account, have the privilege to "spend" the eternal riches of Christ Jesus on those things which He wants us to "buy" in order to extend the kingdom of God on the earth. Again, our desires or whims are not the object of our "purchasing power." The desires of Jesus determine how we appropriate the name of Jesus.

Philippians 2:9-11 describes the position of Jesus with regard to all other powers:

> God has highly exalted Him and given Him the name which is above every name, that at the name of Jesus every knee should bow, of those in heaven, and of those on earth, and of those under the earth, and that every tongue should confess that Jesus Christ is Lord, to the glory of God the Father.

Every name of things above the earth—the spiritual forces of principalities, powers and authorities in the heavenlies.

Every name on the earth—every name associated with human circumstances, including the name of every disease, problem or situation that brings injury, harm or death to human beings.

Every name under the earth—that is, of the forces of hell, including Satan himself.

Jesus has authority over all things so that every tongue, which means every person, might know, understand and proclaim that Jesus Christ is Lord. Jesus has authority over everything, and when we speak in His name—to accomplish His purposes that are for the kingdom of God and against the enemy—this brings forth the greatest witness possible to draw men and women to Christ. That's why "signs and wonders" are so effective in the church. They reveal the lordship of Jesus Christ and the reality that His name is above the name of everything that the enemy causes to come against us or rule over us.

As you live your life, you're always operating under

someone's authority: your parent's authority, your employer's authority, the government's authority. But the Bible tells us in these passages that the authority of Jesus is above all these other types of authority. It doesn't displace them. It doesn't make light of them. But it is more powerful. Just as Luke wrote: We are representing someone "stronger than he"; we represent Jesus, who is stronger than the devil. And when we use the name of Jesus we are always operating under the authority of Jesus.

Notice as you read the book of Acts how many times the apostles healed and worked miracles in the name of Jesus. The name of Jesus was constantly on their lips as they went about proclaiming the gospel, with signs and wonders following.

In Acts 3:6, Peter said to the blind man at the Beautiful Gate, "Silver and gold I do not have, but what I do have I give you: *In the name of Jesus Christ of Nazareth*, rise up and walk" (italics added). And the man immediately began to leap for joy.

In Acts 4:29-30, the apostles prayed: "Lord...grant unto Your servants, that with all boldness they may speak Your word, by stretching out Your hand to heal, and that signs and wonders may be done *through the name of Your holy servant Jesus*" (italics added).

In Acts 16:18, Paul rebuked the demon within a slave girl by saying, "I command you *in the name of Jesus Christ* to come out of her" (italics added). And the demon came out that very hour, freeing this young woman from her bondage.

These are just a few of the incidents in Acts in which the name of Jesus brought forth the authority of Jesus on the earth. Healings, deliverance, blessings—these are the things which Jesus desires for us to purchase on His behalf so that the kingdom of God might be established on the earth, which includes your own life.

The name of Jesus is *your* key to binding the strongman.

It is your strong tower—your high fortress above all the battlefields of the enemy.

Once you act in the power and authority of the name of Jesus, you must next use the Word of God to break those bonds that the strongman has on you. Picture in your mind a man being tied up in ropes. That's the way a spiritual strongman afflicts you. Have you ever heard a person say, "My stomach is all tied up in knots" or "My neck is so stiff it feels like a bunch of knots"? Spiritual bondage is the same way. There's nothing pleasant about it. You feel spiritually tied up in knots, unable to turn and move freely in the Spirit. The ropes of the strongman are cutting into you and causing you pain.

When you declare that Jesus is Lord over your life and not that strongman, you break those bonds. That spiritual "rope" that has been used to tie you up loosens and falls around you. But next comes the moment to take action. You must take up that rope and tie up the strongman himself. You must do to that spiritual strongman the very thing he tried to do to you.

How do you do it? You bind him with the Word of God. Jesus said, "Whatever you bind on earth will be bound in heaven, and whatever you loose on earth will be loosed in heaven" (Matt. 18:18). So you have the power to bind the spiritual force that has held you captive.

If you can't break loose from it and bind it on your own, call a fellow believer in Christ Jesus to help you. Jesus went on to say, "If two of you agree on earth concerning anything that they ask, it will be done for them of My Father in heaven" (Matt. 18:19). Whatever it takes, you need to bind the strongman.

Turn to the strongman and say, "In the name of Jesus, you won't have me any more. I bind your power in the name of Jesus and by the Word of God." And then wrap up that strongman with Scripture verses that declare the righteousness of God in you.

If it's a strongman of fear, you speak directly to it and say, "God has not given me the spirit of fear, but of power and of love and of a sound mind" (see 2 Tim. 1:7). Then say, "Spirit of fear, you will not have any authority over my life. Fear, you are not my lord. Jesus is my Lord. I bind you, spirit of fear. According to the Word of God, I render you powerless and I *resist* you in the name of Jesus."

Say it out loud. Say it as if you mean it. Actually, mean it and then say it! Get tough.

Then ask the Holy Spirit what to do next. He'll give you direction. It might be "go wash the dishes." It might be "sit down and write a letter." It might be "get out of that bed and get dressed and go to work." Whatever it is, set yourself to doing what He says to do.

Whatever the particular spirit might be, you can take the same approach: Find its opposite in the Word of God, and use the Scripture to bind up that strongman.

Spirit of lust? Start declaring, "I have been washed by the blood of Jesus, and even though my sins were as scarlet, they are now as white as snow. (See Is. 1:18.) I've been washed clean and I have a pure heart before God. I've been baptized and my body has been washed by 'pure water.' (See Heb. 10:22.) Therefore, I will put my mind on whatever things are pure and of a good report. Lust, you are not my lord. Jesus is my Lord. You will not have authority over my life. You will not rule my thoughts or my imaginations. In the name of Jesus, get out of my life, and get out now!"

Spirit of loneliness? Say: "You listen up, spirit of loneliness. I have a friend who sticks closer than a brother. (See Prov. 18:24.) His name is Jesus. He has called me friend. (See John 15:15.) He loves me. He cares for me. He watches out for me. And He is here with me now. So, spirit of loneliness, in the name of Jesus, you get out of my life. There's no room for you here. Jesus is my Lord, not you!"

God has dozens of verses of promise and blessing that

you can use to tie up any strongman you can name. Read your Bible and find them. Use a concordance. Ask your Sunday school teacher, home fellowship group leader or pastor to help you find them if you can't find them by yourself. Get prepared.

What about the strongman once he's tied up in the Word of God? Ignore him and walk on. He'll probably try to hobble after you, even in that bound-up state. He doesn't give up easily. If he did, he wouldn't be a *strong* man to begin with.

But remember that when that happens you're facing a critical moment. If you give him your attention, if you allow him to distract you from what the Holy Spirit prompted you to do, then you are, in effect, untying him.

You need to declare once again, "Listen, I thought I told you I didn't have anything to do with you and you don't have anything to do with me. I'm tired of your being around here. Your ways are not my ways. Get out of here!"

You simply refuse to have anything to do with him. He's bound. And if he comes back a second time, which he may very well try to do? Beat him up. Take swift action, in the name of Jesus. Say, "I told you I was through with you. I won't have anything more to do with you. I told you that. Not only do I bind you, I'll punish you for continuing to try to hassle me."

3. Punish the strongman with songs and praises to Jesus.

Sing about the blood of Jesus. Praise God. Declare aloud the glory of God. If you do, that strongman won't hang around. He can't stand to hear about the majesty and glory and wonder of God. He can't stand to hear about the blood of Jesus and the victory of Jesus on the cross. He can't stand to hear about the resurrection power of Jesus over sin, sickness and strife. He can't stand to hear about Jesus' coming back again to this earth to rule and reign. He won't stay around to listen to it.

Don't be satisfied with just binding up that strongman

and walking away. Take authority. Of course, I don't mean authority against any person. This isn't about people at all. We're talking about spiritual warfare. We're talking about wrestling against our spiritual enemy—the devil and his demons. We're talking about taking authority over spiritual wickedness, rulers of darkness, powers and the strongmen that are trying to steal from you every good thing God would have you receive.

If you don't move on into that level of authority—of praising God—then the Scriptures say that you will be worse off than you were at the beginning. (See Luke 11:26.) So I can't begin to tell you how important it is to go on. Once you have identified the strongman coming against you and have declared that he is *not* lord over your life any longer, but that Jesus is Lord; once you have bound that strongman with the Word of God; you must then fill up your mind, your heart and your activities with the Spirit of God.

How do you get filled up with the Spirit of God? You start putting the right things into your spirit. And you keep putting them in again and again. You fill up your mind with new things to think about, the good things of God. You fill up your schedule with new activities, doing works of ministry to help others and enjoying good times of fellowship with the saints of God. You fill up your heart with good feelings that come from giving to others. And you fill up your spirit with the Word of God in song and in spoken word.

You listen to praise music, including the praise music you make with your own lips. You listen to the Word of God being preached with power, and you preach it to yourself, meditating on it, memorizing it, declaring it to yourself as you drive down the highway or shower in the morning. You read the Scriptures aloud so your own mind can hear it and receive it. Singing and declaring the praises of God this way will build you up.

173

Picture a person all bound in ropes by the strongman. Then picture how he got free by declaring Jesus to be Lord. Picture how he bound up the strongman with the Word of God. But now that person who was once bound needs to limber up. He needs to move. He may have been bound up a long time and now he needs to stretch his muscles and get some strength back.

That's the position you're in once you've bound a spiritual strongman in your life. You're free. He's bound. But now you need to get the strength to pummel that strongman into the ground. Remember what King David said about his enemy: "I beat them as fine as the dust of the earth; I trod them like dirt in the street, and I spread them out" (2 Sam. 22:43). So beat that strongman into dust by declaring the Word of God. Stamp him into the mud by singing praises to God.

Remember, I'm not talking about human enemies. There are three things you should do to human enemies, and only three things:

1) Love them.
2) Bless them.
3) Do something good for them.

That's it. That's our agenda for *human beings* who come against us. When we do that, God will return a blessing to us. Their very efforts to destroy us will be thwarted by God Himself. We don't need to worry about it or even give it a second thought.

But our agenda against spiritual wickedness is to identify the strongmen, combat them with the full force of our strength in Christ, and destroy them, crush them, annihilate them. We're on a spiritual search-and-destroy mission against the powers of darkness.

There's absolutely *no* place in the Word of God where it says that you are to be kind to Satan. There's *no* place where it says you are to have mercy on demon powers. There is *no* place where it says your kindness must extend to spiritual wickedness. There is *no* place where it says that you are to be patient with the rulers of darkness. There is *no* place where you are commanded to extend the least bit of love toward the demonic enemy who is coming to steal from you, destroy you and kill you.

Be kind to people. But get mean with the devil. Be loving to people. But destroy demons. Be longsuffering with people. But pummel the rulers of darkness, the powers, the spiritual wickedness and the forces of evil all around you. Be merciful to people. But tear up the enemy.

Put the strongman to flight. Get him on the run. And if you catch him, pummel him into the earth. This is hand-to-hand combat for your personal life, your family, your church, your city, your nation.

That means taking on one stronghold and pulling it down. Then moving on to the next stronghold and pulling it down. And then the next, and the next, and the next. You must become a warrior on the offensive, winning a battle and then marching on to the next battle even as you're rejoicing in the victory.

Declare today: Jesus is Lord over my life. No other power will have even a toehold. This stronghold coming against my life through the lust of the flesh, the lust of the eyes or the pride of life (1 John 2:16) has no authority over me any more, beginning this moment. Jesus is Lord and He is the only Lord of my life.

I bind the strongman in my life with the name of Jesus and the Word of God. Spirit of anger, I bind you in the name of Jesus. Spirit of selfishness, I bind you in the name of Jesus. Spirit of pride, I bind you in the name of Jesus. You will not rule my life. I resist you and you must flee. I am free by Jesus Christ.

I sing the praises of God. I declare His Word. I release the spirit of love into my life. I release the spirit of courage. I release the spirit of obedience. I *will* walk in the Spirit of God.

Taking What Is Rightfully Yours

Now the enemy is not only coming at you to bind you up and to keep you from being and doing all that God desires for you. The enemy is also at work to keep you from having all that God desires for you.

Look at God's promise in Isaiah 43:4-7:

> Since you were precious in My sight, you have been honored, and I have loved you; therefore I will give men for you, and people for your life. Fear not, for I am with you, I will bring your descendants from the east, and gather you from the west; I will say to the north, 'Give them up!' and to the south, 'Do not keep them back!' Bring My sons from afar, and My daughters from the ends of the earth—everyone who is called by My name, whom I have created for My glory; I have formed him, yes, I have made him.

"Since you were precious in My sight." You are precious to the Lord. He paid the price of His Son, Jesus Christ, on the cross for you. You were purchased by the blood of Jesus. You are precious to God.

"You have been honored, and I have loved you." You have been made the righteousness of God. You have walked in His ways. You have sought as your first priority walking in the victory of the Holy Spirit. And the Lord loves you. You are His son, His daughter.

"I will give men for you, and people for your life." God wants to surround you with the people you need to help you with your work, to encourage you, to prosper you, to build you up in the faith. Luke 6:39 says that God gives back to the giver such abundance that even when it is shaken together and pressed down, it will run over and that "men will give to your bosom."

God doesn't rain down money from heaven. Coins don't fall from the sky like raindrops. God's method is to work through people. And God says that He will give you the people you need surrounding you to help you fight your fights, pay your bills, provide work for you, be your friends and pray with you—to meet the needs in every area of your life.

In the area of financial prosperity, He will give you the clients you need, the vendors, the distributors, the salesmen. He'll give you patients, students, colleagues. He'll give you the employer you need, the right contacts, the best banker. He'll give you "people."

"Fear not." Don't allow disbelief or fear to overwhelm you because what the Lord is about to say will come to pass. And He will bring these resources to you from the East, West, North and South—even from the ends of the earth.

At the Church on the Rock, when we pray together that phrase of the Lord's prayer that says, "Thy kingdom come, thy will be done, on earth as it is in heaven," we stand and turn to the North and say, "North, give up what belongs to this church." Then we turn to the East and say, "East, give up what belongs to this church." We turn to the South and to the West and say the same thing. We want everything that God wants to give us. We cry, "Give up, enemy, what belongs to us. Don't hold back, enemy, what is ours."

Now this refers to everything that God wants us to have. It means resources and blessings for our individual lives. It means souls being saved in our churches because sinners are coming in and hearing the Word of God preached with power. It means resources coming into our churches. It means every miracle that we need coming our way.

One reason the strongman comes to bind you is to keep you from receiving those things that God wants to send your way. So our job is to claim those things as our own.

As the Church on the Rock grew in numbers, the Lord revealed to me in my times of prayer that my primary job as a pastor was to break through the spiritual darkness over Rockwall and over the lives of those He wanted to bring into our congregation. I knew beyond any shadow of a doubt that great preaching wouldn't cause souls to be saved and the church to grow. Finely honed theology spelled out in precise statements wouldn't do it. No, only the tearing down of strongholds that were holding back the people from experiencing God in their lives would cause the church to grow.

So I went to the church building on Saturday nights to pray especially for the services the next day. Often I met others there, but on one particular Saturday night I was alone. The church auditorium was dark, with only one light on above the baptistry in front.

As I knelt there and cried aloud to the Lord, I broke through into a spiritual dimension that I don't know how to describe for you. I was in "rarified air" spiritually speaking. When I declared to the North, South, East and West to give up what belongs to the Church on the Rock, I felt a presence in that auditorium that was unlike anything I had ever experienced. And it was *not* a holy presence.

I was kneeling with my eyes closed, and at that moment when I felt this presence in the room, I looked up and in my spiritual vision I saw a being standing in front of me. He was holding a large silver chain in his hands. I'll never forget it as long as I live.

My first impulse was to get up and run out of the building. But at the same time, I knew that I was at a moment of truth, a divine intersection. I realized that I was face-to-face with the very power that was holding back the harvest of souls that God wanted to bring into the Church on the Rock.

The being communicated to me these words, "Do you really mean it? Are you serious? Are you really going to take your stand?"

Immediately that inner Man within me—the One the Scriptures refer to as "greater...than he that is in the world"—stood up. Before I knew what I was doing, I literally stood to my feet and shouted back at this being, "You're mighty right I mean what I'm saying!"

I stepped toward him, and when I did, he stepped back. I knew I had him on the run. He dropped the chain and disappeared. He was gone.

From that day to this, I have never encountered anything like that again. But in the next twelve months, we saw some thirty-four hundred people walk the aisles of the Church on the Rock getting saved or uniting with our church. We held no special revivals. We conducted no house-to-house canvasses. We sponsored no special membership drives. It happened solely by the power of God shining through the powers of darkness. The strongman had been bound and the kingdom of God released.

Something new is emerging in the spirit realm today. God is calling His church to rise up and become militant warriors who will stand and say to principalities and powers, "Yes, we are taking a stand. Yes, we mean it. Yes, we declare to you that you will not have our children; you will not have our families; you will not have our churches; you will not have our blessings." And we will drive back the darkness so that the glory of God might shine more strongly.

God's desire is for you to pray this way. Believe it!

What's the purpose of prayer anyway? Prayer is not coming to God to convince Him to do something He doesn't want to do. Prayer is coming into agreement with God about something He already wants to do. It's saying, "I'll do my part so that You, Lord, are free to do Your part."

God's desire is that you have all He wants you to have and experience all He wants you to experience for your spiritual good. Sometimes we don't think big enough. Sometimes we don't expect enough. Sometimes we don't desire His blessings nearly to the extent that He wants to give them.

I remember one time when I was praying and calling out

to the North, South, East and West. God spoke in my spirit and said, "You're turning to the North, but in your spirit you're only getting as far as Denton. And when you turn to the East, you're believing only as far as Greenville out in east Texas. Son, I'm the God of the whole world. When I turn to the East, I'm looking as far as *Germany!*"

The very next Sunday, I gave an invitation to people to join the church, and down the aisle walked a beautiful couple with their children. The Lord prompted me to stop them and ask them where they were from. The father stopped, clicked his heels, saluted me and said, "My name is Lieutenant Bob Cooper, and I was stationed in Germany when I got your tapes on prayer. God told me to resign my commission in the military, which I've had for nine years, and move to Rockwall to report for duty."

My soul nearly soared out of my body when that man said "Germany." I knew that I was standing in the heart of something very big. God has vast blessings for His people—there are no limits. But we must break through the darkness to let the kingdom come shining through. When you break through the spiritual powers and the glory of God starts to shine through, you don't have to do much preaching to get folks saved.

We had a musical at our church recently and the choir and orchestra were magnificent. But the greatest part of the service was watching some eighty people walk the aisle to accept Jesus Christ into their lives. My wife and I have grown up around great musicals all our lives. But most of the time, we've noticed that after a great evening performance by the choir, everybody "oohs" and "aahs" a bit, then they all fall silent while the pastor stands and leads the singing of "Just As I Am." Maybe one or two come forward at the most.

Our musical wasn't technically any better than those performed at most other places. The difference was that the choir was singing with the sun shining on them from heaven. The spiritual darkness had been punctured so that the glory of God could come through. Those who had prayed and interceded before God, not just that day, but every day at sunrise for year after year, had cleared the space. They had pushed back the powers of evil so that the kingdom of God might be established. And it was! Without a great effort. Without singing "Just As I Am" ten times through. Without pleading. Eighty people accepted Jesus as Savior and Lord that one night. Now that's the kind of miracle that happens when the enemy is forced, by our taking a stand in prayer, to give up what belongs to God almighty.

We are to stand strong in the honor, love and courage of God and cry out, "Give up, enemies to the North, everything God has for me, for my family, for my church. Give up, enemies of the South, everything God has for me, for my family, for my church. Give up, enemies of the East, everything God has for me, for my family and for my church. Give up, enemies of the West, everything God has for me, for my family and for my church. Give it up! It's mine! It's ours."

God says, "I'll do it. If you'll speak to the enemy like that, I'll do My part. I'll cause things to come your way. It will happen."

When you declare these things, believe that they are done on earth as they are in heaven. When you start to fight battles like that, winning them for the Lord, though the world situation gets darker and darker, you'll shine brighter and brighter. As those in the world feel worse and worse, you'll be feeling better and better. As the world's systems get weaker and weaker, you'll grow stronger and stronger. As the world starts winding down, you'll be winding up. Instead of wondering what will happen next, you'll be asking, "Where's the next victory, Lord?"

Give God the glory, for the great works He has done, is doing and will do. The victory is ours. It's yours. It's mine. It's a sure victory if we'll but fight the fight.

Close the Door on the Devil Today

1) What things are lording it over you? Write them out in a list.

2) Write an appropriate verse of Scripture next to each item you listed above.

3) Now place your hand over that list and declare aloud: "In the name of Jesus, I declare that Jesus is Lord, not this problem. Jesus is the Lord of *all* my life, including this circumstance. The name of Jesus is mightier than:

_____

(the name of the problem, disease, circumstance or situation)

4) Declare aloud: "This is the truth of the situation, devil. Let me read the Word of God to you one more time." Then read aloud your verses of Scripture.

5) Ask God to give you specific direction about what to do. Write down what God impresses you to do.

6) Place your hand over this word of instruction to you from the Holy Spirit and declare aloud: "I will do this and trust God to free me totally from this strongman."

7) Praise Jesus. Declare everything that He is and that He does for you, what He has been and had done, what He will be and will do. Wear out the devil with your praises until you feel a release in your spirit from the bondage you've felt.

8) Why not write your name in the space below as a lasting reminder of your freedom in Christ Jesus, beginning right this hour?

_____

(Your name here)
Free in Christ Jesus!

Let's pray and agree together you'll never forget that you can bind the strongman with the name of Jesus and the Word of God: "In the name of Jesus, I agree with you that this word is sealed forever in my heart and in my life. I declare today that I am free of the strongman that has been harassing me. I praise You, heavenly Father. I exalt You. I lift up the name of Jesus on the earth. I bless You, Jesus Christ. I proclaim You as victor, Lord, Savior, deliverer, redeemer, soon-coming king! I stand on Your word today that I am free in Christ Jesus! Amen."

TEN

Finishing Strong!

Not long ago, a man phoned me who was very upset. He was a Christian who had just come from a restaurant where he had witnessed a man bowing his head in prayer before he began eating. Being very impressed that this man was bold enough to ask God's blessing on his meal so openly in such a nice restaurant, he had excused himself from his friends who were at the table with him, and he had gone over to the man to let him know how much his actions had encouraged him.

He got the shock of his life.

"I wasn't asking God to bless my food," the man said. "I was praying to Satan. And I was praying that Satan will destroy the top churches and ministries across this nation during the coming months."

"You're praying this all by yourself?" the Christian muttered, trying to be a little objective in order to ease some of the tension he felt in his spirit.

"Oh, no," the satanist laughed. "There are thousands of us organized across the nation. We've agreed to pray diligently for this to happen *until it does!*"

The Christian was so shaken by what he'd heard that he could hardly tell me the story without stuttering.

185

Does this story frighten you? Does it compel you to take action? I pray that it does! While the enemy isn't as powerful as many people think, the enemy *is* far more clever, far more organized and far more persistent than many of us give him credit for being.

What then must we do? We must lift up Jesus even higher. We must stand up and be counted among God's warriors. We must prepare ourselves in the Lord, experience His blood, put on the whole armor of God, voice our battle cry and scale the enemy fortresses to pull down those principalities, thrones and powers of darkness in active spiritual combat. And we must do it "to the end."

Revelation 12:11 concludes: "And they overcame him by the blood of the Lamb and by the word of their testimony, *and they did not love their lives to the death.*" In other words, they were willing to put it all on the line. They were willing to give their all. This was a cause—as David said before he went down to meet Goliath—worthy of total sacrifice.

Who Are You?

In recent months we've experienced a number of trials and difficulties at the Church on the Rock where I have pastored since January 1980—the home base of our prayer army. I haven't been surprised. If I were the enemy, I'd try to stop, abort, hold back, malign or push down the mission of the Church on the Rock any way I could. I've noticed something through the years of my ministry. It isn't the weak soldiers of God who are the most persecuted. It isn't the timid soldiers of God who have all hell thrown against them. I know the Church on the Rock is going to be assaulted, and I praise God that the enemy considers us such a threat.

But I also know something else on which I've staked my life: I know Jesus Christ. I know Jesus Christ is Lord. I know

186

Jesus Christ is Savior. I know Jesus Christ is deliverer. I know Jesus Christ is victor. I also know that if I cling to Jesus, choose to live in Him and seek to have Him live out His life through me, then this battle and every other battle are His battles. And my Bible says that they are "good battles" because He wins.

Therefore, despite the attacks of the devil, I'm not bitter. I'm better. I'm not weak. I'm ready to march. I'm not tired. I'm strong. I'm not discouraged. I'm encouraged that I've been given a commission from the Lord Jesus Christ. I've been told to stand up. I've been told to fight the good fight in the spiritual realm. Yet it's not I, but Christ within me. (See Gal. 2:20.)

I'm not some broken-down, weak, insipid preacher groveling around, trying to get a little something done over in one corner. No way! I'm God's battle-ax.

I'm not just an old dog out here, trying to live the best I can through this old troubled world. Not this man! I'm God's instrument—a tool He has raised up to fight spiritual battles and win.

I'm not standing in my own armor. I have on the armor of God. I'm not standing in my own strength. I'm standing in the strength of Jesus Christ. I'm not standing in my own reputation or in my good works or in my accomplishments. No, I'm standing in the righteousness of Jesus Christ, whose shed blood purchased for me my rights to the kingdom of God and its peace and joy. And so do you.

Who are you today? What did you say to yourself in the mirror this morning? Did you greet yourself with a look of despair or a look of joy? Did you greet yourself with words of gloom or words of peace? Did you say, "I'm just a poor ol' sinner struggling to get by" or did you say, "I'm the righteousness of God in Christ Jesus"?

The Lines Have Been Drawn

The lines for the final showdown have already been drawn. The days are over when you can be what I call a "Leave-It-to-Beaver" Christian, living some nice little life, going to church on Sunday mornings and not having any apparent struggles with the forces of darkness.

Remember: The devil has a plan for your life and it's a lousy one. It's one that's meant for your despair, death and destruction. You'll either walk in victory or you'll have demons hanging all over you and your family. You'll either be an overcomer or you'll be overcome. You'll either be in the winner's circle or you'll be utterly wiped out. So the time has come to stand tall and move forward and to be committed to fighting the good fight *to the end*.

God Is a Finisher

God has never started anything He intends to leave unfinished. Get that truth buried deep in your heart and let it live within you. God is a finisher.

God started with humanity in the Garden of Eden, and ever since, He's been busy finishing what He began. The nation of Israel took a side road through their disobedience, but God *will* finish what He began in the nation of Israel.

The Lord Jesus Christ came on the scene obsessed with the burning passion to finish what God gave Him to do. At one point in His ministry He said, "My food is to do the will of Him who sent me, and to finish His work" (see John 4:34). *Finishing* was what motivated Jesus. It's what kept Him going even when times got tough and the persecution mounted against Him. His attitude was "I must finish. I must do My work."

The final three words Jesus said before He died on the cross were "It is finished." He accomplished what was set before Him to do. He got the job done.

That "spirit of a finisher" is also something the apostle

Paul had. A man by the name of Agabus prophesied over the apostle Paul one day and said, "If you go to Jerusalem"—which was the will of God for Paul—"you'll have chains put on you. You'll be taken into custody, bound and turned over to the Gentiles." (See Acts 21:10-11.) Every implication drawn from this prophecy points toward Paul's death in custody.

But Paul, when he heard these words, didn't respond out of fear. He didn't turn aside from his journey. He said, "I am ready not only to be bound, but also to die at Jerusalem for the name of the Lord Jesus" (Acts 21:13).

This same Paul also said, "But none of these things moves me; nor do I count my life dear to myself, so that I may finish my race with joy, and the ministry, which I received from the Lord Jesus, to testify to the gospel of the grace of God" (Acts 20:24).

Paul was obsessed with the desire to finish everything that God put before him to do. He wrote to the Philippian church while he was a prisoner in Rome, "Brethren, I do not count myself to have apprehended"—[in other words, he was saying "I don't know everything there is to know"]—'but one thing I do'—[and notice that word *do*]—"forgetting those things which are behind and reaching forward to those things which are ahead, I press toward the goal for the prize of the upward call of God in Christ Jesus" (Phil. 3:14).

Paul had a press-forward mind-set. It wasn't enough for the apostle Paul to be saved and get started in his Christian walk. He had a heart that desired to press on in his Christian walk, to go somewhere in his faith, to do everything that he could do to have more of Jesus, extend the kingdom and win spiritual battles for God.

Paul also wrote his godson, Timothy, from his prison cell in Rome as his life was drawing to a close: "I have fought the good fight, I have finished the race, I have kept the faith" (2 Tim. 4:7). The bottom line of his life was this:

"I got the job done. I finished!" And we're called to have this same "spirit of a finisher."

Death won't be a big deal for me—if I finish my course. Stop to think about it. What's the worst thing that can happen to you for telling others about Jesus and for fighting spiritual battles?

"I could die!" you say. And what's so terrible about that? You'll get to be with Jesus and to experience life everlasting in His presence. No more pain, no more sorrows, no more disappointments, no more hardships.

No, I think there's something worse than dying for the faith. It's dying without finishing your course. It's dying with regret about what might have been.

What a terrible thing it would be for me to get to the end of my life and have to say, "I know what You called me to do, God, but I didn't do it." I can't think of anything worse than that.

We'll face God one day and He'll say, "I gave you skills, talents, opportunities and resources. What did you do with them? Where did it all go? How did you spend your time? How did you use your resources? How did you invest the years I gave you on the earth?"

On that day the cry of our hearts will be, "God, be merciful!" And He will be merciful. Everyone who calls on the name of the Lord will be saved. But if we haven't finished the course He set before us, we won't experience the rewards He desires to give us.

I want to be able to stand before God and say, "Lord, here's a nation for You! Here are sheep that were saved as a result of my staying true to the course You set before me. I didn't give up in the face of adversity. I didn't give up when the devil tempted me to give up. I didn't stop when people told me that I had done enough and I should rest on my laurels. I kept the faith, and now by Your grace I'm finishing my course!"

God is a finisher. Jesus is a finisher. The Spirit of God,

that same spirit that was in Christ Jesus, is a finisher—and He lives within you today. So you must become a finisher.

I read the end of the book—the Bible, I mean—and it says that God is a finisher. Jesus really will come again. He really will take the devil and lock him in a bottomless pit. He really will rule and reign in this world. We really will reign on it with Him. A new heaven and a new earth really will be established. We really will reign with Jesus forever and ever.

You may wonder whether or not you're able to do it. You may ask whether or not you'll be able to stand strong for the Lord all your life and to finish your course. But just read God's promises to you throughout the Bible.

Philippians 1:6: "Being confident of this very thing, that He who has begun a good work in you will complete it until the day of Jesus Christ." Be confident! Jesus will finish in you the work that He has begun. He won't turn you loose. He won't abandon you. He will cause those things in your life to be resolved for good, to come to fruition, and to bear an eternal harvest. You can stake everything on it. Take Him as your confidence today.

Psalm 138:8: "The Lord will perfect that which concerns me; Your mercy, O Lord, endures forever." God will complete it. He'll continue the growth in you until it comes to fruition in due season. He'll stick with you. He'll endure by your side and never leave you. In that same psalm—Psalm 138—we read that the Lord will walk with you in the midst of your troubles. He'll revive you when you faint. He'll defeat your enemies when they come against you. And He'll uphold you with His right hand, which means with His strength. What a promise to you!

First Thessalonians 5:23 says: "Now may the God of peace Himself sanctify you completely; and may your whole spirit, soul, and body be preserved blameless at the coming of our Lord Jesus Christ. He who calls you is faithful, who also will do it." You will be made whole. God is faithful to do that work in you. He's faithful. Shout it aloud: "God is faithful!"

Every time we come to Him saying, "God, I turn from my sins, I turn from my failures, I turn from my shortcomings; help me to follow in Your footsteps and to walk in Your paths of righteousness," He's faithful to hear and answer that prayer.

Do you recall in the Bible the story of the prodigal son and how the father responds when the young man returns home? (See Luke 15:11-31.) The father jumps up and runs to greet him! That's the way the Lord responds to our prayers for forgiveness and to our desire to follow after Him, to seek His kingdom and His will with all our hearts. He runs toward us. He's just waiting for the opportunity to show His faithfulness and His enduring mercies.

Gaining the Spirit of a Finisher

What does it take to have the heart of a finisher? What are the attributes of a finisher? What makes for the spirit of a finisher?

I believe a finisher has five attributes which we should remember as we close out this book. They're drawn from 1 Peter 5:5-10. Read these verses carefully as they appear in the Amplified Bible:

> Likewise you that are younger and of lesser rank be subject to the elders—the ministers and spiritual guides of the church, giving them due respect and yielding to their counsel. Clothe (apron) yourselves, all of you with humility—as the garb of a servant, so that its covering cannot possibly be stripped from you, with freedom from pride and arrogance— toward one another. For God sets Himself against the proud—the insolent, the overbearing, the disdainful, the presumptuous, the boastful, and opposes, frustrates and defeats them—but gives grace

(favor, blessing) to the humble.

Therefore, humble yourselves (demote, lower yourselves in your own estimation) under the mighty hand of God that in due time He may exalt you.

Casting the whole of your care—all your anxieties, all your worries, all your concerns once and for all—on Him, for He cares for you affectionately, and cares about you watchfully.

Be well-balanced, temperate, sober-minded; be vigilant and cautious at all times, for that enemy of yours, the devil, roams around like a lion roaring [in fierce hunger], seeking someone to seize upon and devour.

Withstand him; be firm in faith [against his onset],—rooted, established, strong, immovable and determined—knowing that the same (identical) sufferings are appointed to your brotherhood (the whole body of Christians) throughout the world.

And after you have suffered a little while, the God of all grace—Who imparts all blessing and favor—Who has called you to His [own] eternal glory in Christ Jesus, will Himself complete and make you what you ought to be, establish and ground you securely, and strengthen (and settle) you.

Jesus Is Your All in All

If you would be a finisher, the first attribute you must have is that Jesus must be the absolute Lord of your life. Jesus must be top priority—in fact, your only priority. He must become and remain your only source of security in this life. That is the supreme hallmark of the man or woman who has the "spirit of a finisher."

If Jesus is not the Lord of your life, you are a joke to the devil. You make him laugh when you invoke the blood of Jesus, the name of Jesus, the weapons of our warfare, unless

Jesus is truly Lord to you. The devil knows the score.

He knows that on one side of the cross lie the kingdom of darkness and the kingdom of the world. You'll find the devil and his minions on that side, with all their deceptions, death, hatred, poverty, sickness, meanness, greed, pride, arrogance and the systems of this world.

On the other side of the cross are the kingdom of God and the kingdom of light and righteousness. That's where you'll find Jesus and the angels of God. On that side are peace, joy, freedom, liberty, love, power, healing, prosperity, righteousness.

In between is the cross. And on the cross it says, "If any man come after Jesus and believe Him, let him deny himself and take up his cross daily, and follow Jesus." (See Mark 8:34.)

So many of us miss it at this point. We say, "The heart of the gospel is that we are to come to the cross, believe Jesus, go join a church and then live any way we want to live." Isn't that the atttitude of most of us, even those of us who claim to be Christians?

But that isn't what the Scriptures say. They say we are to deny ourselves. We're to say no to greed, pride, hate, lust, selfishness and the sinfulness of our flesh. And until we're ready to do that, we won't be saved.

Let's say it another way. You're not "saved" until you come to the place in your life where you're ready to exchange your life in the flesh for a cross that says you're dead to sin. You really have only one right. It's the right to embrace the cross of Jesus with all your being and say, "Jesus, what next?" That's the only right you have in this world from heaven's point of view.

As Paul wrote to the Galatians: "I am crucified with Christ: nevertheless I live, yet not I, but Christ liveth in me: and the life which I now live in the flesh I live by the faith of the Son of God, who loved me, and gave himself for me" (Gal. 2:20, KJV).

We don't live for ourselves. We don't live for this world. We live in Christ, for Christ, because of Christ. That requires what I call the "great exchange." It requires a total change of heart, a total change of perspective, a total change of priority. It requires exchanging life in this world for life in Jesus.

Jesus said to the rich young ruler, "Go, sell everything you have and give it to the poor, and in doing that, you'll have treasure in heaven"—in other words, you'll have everything that has any true worth. (See Mark 10:17-22.) But the rich young ruler wasn't willing to make the great exchange. Zacchaeus, on the other hand, said, "Lord, half my goods I give to the poor and if I've taken anything from any man by false means, I'll restore it fourfold." He was willing to make the great exchange, and Jesus said, "Today salvation has come to your house, Zacchaeus." (See Luke 19:1-9.)

It's tough to make the great exchange. Many people are hung up on the stuff they own. The devil has convinced them that their stuff is reality. They base their security in life on how many "toys" they have. They've bought into the attitude that "he who dies with the most toys wins."

But that's not what Jesus taught. Jesus taught that there is no security outside of your relationship with Him. There is no other reality, no other means of righteousness, no other foundation for life that is lasting. The only things we can truly count on are the lordship of Jesus Christ and His absolute victory over the devil.

The first mark of the person who has the "spirit of a finisher" is the mark of total commitment to the lordship of Jesus. It's grasping the cross for dear life and trusting Him, and Him alone, to be Lord. As the passage from 1 Peter says:

> The God of all grace—Who imparts all blessing and favor—Who has called you to His [own] eternal

195

THE WEAPONS OF YOUR WARFARE

glory in Christ Jesus, will Himself complete and make you what you ought to be; establish and ground you securely, and strengthen (and settle) you.

Stay in Fellowship

The second attribute of a finisher is submission to the covering of a local church. No one finishes alone. Your ability to finish is rooted in your relationship with others in the body of Christ.

People who have the spirit of a finisher also have the spirit of staying power within the body of Christ. They don't give up when things get tough. They don't let a disagreement over differences separate them from their church leaders or other fellow Christians. They don't let one point of doctrine turn them away from regular church attendance.

I live my life today under the authority of the laws of this land. Those laws are made, interpreted and administered by the leaders of our nation—the president, the Congress and the Supreme Court. I have a choice: I can stay under that authority, leave the country and lose all the privileges and benefits of being an American or break the law. I choose to stay under authority. That doesn't mean I agree 100 percent with every law. That doesn't mean I agree with the leadership style of every political leader in our nation or that I agree completely with my particular senator or congressman. It doesn't mean I agree 100 percent with the president. But I have respect for their offices and for their authority within this nation.

That's how it works in the church. You will never agree 100 percent of the time, in every situation or circumstance. But in the passage from 1 Peter 5:5 we read, "Likewise you that are younger and of lesser rank be subject to the elders—the ministers and spiritual guides of the church, giving them due respect and yielding to their counsel" (Amplified). It's just not possible as human beings to reach total agreement. But you can make a decision that you will "agree in the Lord."

Spiritual agreement involves a choice to remain under the authority of your local church leaders. It means that you choose to agree on the things that are important—the blood of Jesus, the lordship of Jesus, the first priority of Jesus in your lives.

Remember: You'll never find the "right" preacher or fellowship by hopping from one church to another year after year. I've met people who have gone to ten different churches in the past three years. My advice is to get within a local church body and stay there. Put down roots. Work to make that church a body of people that loves one another, works together to extend the gospel and treats one another with respect. And leave it only if the Holy Spirit leads you to another place of service or growth.

The person who decides to walk away from the church, to stand alone and to cry, "Come on, devil, try to get me" is asking for trouble. The Bible says that "where two or more are gathered in My name" is the place where you'll find Jesus at work. That's where you'll find the signs and wonders of the Holy Spirit in operation. That's where you'll find comfort and love in times of crisis.

Stay in fellowship with other Spirit-filled believers. That's the second great hallmark of the man or woman who has the spirit of a finisher.

Cast Away All Your Worry

The third attribute of a finisher is a complete and lasting decision about worry. We discussed this at length earlier in this book, but we must repeat it here: Worry is a completely alien concept to the man or woman of God who bears the spirit of a finisher.

Once again from 1 Peter 5:7 we read: "Casting the whole of your care—all your anxieties, all your worries, all your concerns, once and for all—on Him, for He cares for you affectionately, and cares about you watchfully'' (Amplified).

The *whole* of your care. *All* of your anxiety. *All* of your worries. *All* of your concerns. Once and for all.

I know some Christians who worry so much that if they didn't worry, they'd start to worry about not worrying! If we hold onto a problem with our worry and don't give it to the Lord, then the Lord can't do anything about it. But if we cast all of our concern about a tough situation onto Him, then He can deal with it.

Look at the relationship described in this passage from 1 Peter. It says Jesus cares for us affectionately. In other words, Jesus isn't going to laugh at us or look down on us for casting our cares onto Him. He loves us when we pour our problems out to Him and ask Him to carry our burdens and deal with them. He is affectionate, or tender-hearted, toward us when we admit that we can't deal with a situation and ask Him to step in. This is something Jesus wants us to do. It isn't a bother to Him. It doesn't weigh Him down. On the contrary, it frees Him up to resolve the problem.

When you're hit with a problem, don't hang your head and cry, ''What will I do now?'' Instead, raise your head to heaven and cry, ''God, You said You'll finish what You began in me. You said that everything was working out a process for good in my life. You said You'd bring me to completion so that when You look at me, I'll look more and more like Jesus to You. Now here's my problem.''

The men and women of God who have the spirit of a finisher have their eyes on the goal. They see what God can do, what God wants to do and what God will do. They don't get bogged down in worry over past or present circumstances. They pray over their circumstances with faith believing God to resolve those circumstances. They listen for what God directs them to do. And then they march forward in their lives to do what He says.

"Cast all your worry on Jesus." That's the third hallmark of the person who is a finisher.

You Live in a War Zone

The fourth attribute of finishers is that they never lose sight of the fact that they're in a war. You are a warrior. You are a part of the church militant that is becoming the church triumphant. You are God's battle-ax.

The days are long past when we can be casual about the spirit realm. The days are over when we can be casual in our faith, casual in our giving or casual in the way we think about God and heaven.

So many people seem to treat God as if He's a commodity they can take or leave. They think they can buy a little religion, keep it over in one compartment and take it or leave it at their own leisure and in their own time.

But that's not the way it is. We must accept what the apostle Peter wrote as true for us today: "Be well-balanced—temperate, sober-minded; be vigilant and cautious at all times, for that enemy of yours, the devil, roams around like a lion roaring [in fierce hunger], seeking someone to seize upon and devour. Withstand him; be firm in faith against his onset" (1 Peter 5:8-9, Amplified).

In other words, get serious! Be sober-minded about the war at hand. Recognize the battle for what it is—an attack rooted in a spiritual war.

Don't fly off in a panic. On the other hand, don't stick your head in the sand. Be *balanced* in what you do.

Stay on the alert. Always. Be aware that the enemy is coming at you all the time. He's coming at you with a roar that will put fear in your heart if you're not on the alert. What's one of the greatest causes of fear, the kind that erupts into panic? It's being taken by surprise. The apostle Peter is saying, "Don't be surprised when the devil roars at you. It's his nature to stalk you. It's his nature to be hungry for one more human being to destroy or kill.'' Don't be surprised when the devil acts like the devil.

Then Peter says to withstand. Put on your whole armor of God every day. Resist his temptations. Put up your shield of faith to divert his fiery darts. Pray always in the Spirit. Don't just expect the devil to come around and harass you. Expect Jesus to be there to fight with you to victory. Expect to come home from the battle to a hero's welcome with all of heaven standing at attention and applauding what Jesus has done in you and through you.

Expect to keep your marriage together and to love your spouse. Expect to see your children grow up strong and healthy, not on drugs or in immorality. Expect to see your church grow and add new souls to the kingdom of God and to see those in bondage delivered by the power of the Holy Spirit. Expect to see your business or your job prosper and grow. Expect Jesus Christ to be Lord in every circumstance you face. *Expect to win!*

The fourth great hallmark of men and women with the spirit of a finisher is that they're on the alert for the enemy, and they're prepared to withstand his assault.

A Desire to Win and Only to Win

The fifth attribute of finishers is that they decide every morning when their feet hit the ground that they won't settle for second place or mere survival. You must decide that you'll win.

You must decide that when your life is over, you'll be one who stands before God and says, ''I have fought and I have won.'' You must decide that even though the battle might be fierce, when the smoke clears away and bodies are lying all around, you'll still be standing upright.

One Christmas morning several years ago, my dad and I were talking in our living room about his experiences in World War II. He was in the ''C'' Company of the 82nd

Airborne Division, and at one time "C" Company fought for more than three hundred days in a row without a break. "C" Company was replaced 300 percent during the war, which means that the equivalent of the entire company was killed and replaced three times. My dad was one of only a handful that got out of "C" Company alive.

"Dad," I asked, "I want to know how you kept fighting. What kept you going?"

My dad looked at me soberly and said, "We had to win."

I said, "What do you mean?"

He repeated, "We *had* to win."

"Why did you believe that so strongly?"

"Well, son, I thought about Hitler and about the Third Reich. Then I thought about my mother and brothers and sisters living under the dominion of Adolf Hitler. And I knew we *had* to win. There was no alternative."

Today you and I fight an enemy who is more real, more lethal and more evil than anyone in World War II. He is at war today with you and me and this great nation of ours in a way that's far more deadly and oppressive than the war my dad experienced from 1941 to 1945.

Stop to think what happens if we don't fight to win. What happens to your children—and to their children—should the Lord delay His coming that long?

I'm fighting to pull down strongholds because I don't want John Aaron, Joanna, Joy Elizabeth and their children and their children's children to receive a form of religion that lulls them to sleep and is without power. I don't want them to experience the oppression of the enemy so that it overwhelms them from all sides. I don't want them to be blinded by a church that calls wrong right, and right, wrong.

I'm in this fight to win. I'm not just trying to tiptoe through the tulips or to avoid making waves. We have a battle to win, and the alternative is losing—losing not just a little bit here and there, but losing everything; and not just for a little while, but forever.

Today I'm asking you, I'm pleading with you, I'm exhorting you: Wake up to the real situation you face. You have an enemy. You're in a war. Your eternal life and your present life are at stake.

Get a warrior's mentality.

Start applying the blood of Jesus to every circumstance of your life.

Seek God as your first priority, your spiritual reveille every morning.

Learn how to march in victory, praying your covenant promises before God, standing on your faith as He directs your steps, and praising Him with a loud voice.

Get a word of testimony and then shout it as your battle cry. Know what you believe and be bold in proclaiming it.

Resolve within you that the battle is worth winning. Don't shy away from the fight. Bind the strongman. Use your prayer power to puncture the clouds of darkness so that the sunshine light of almighty God can shine forth on the earth. Take up your weapons of spiritual warfare and be an overcomer.

Fight until the fight is over. Have the spirit of a finisher, trusting in Jesus fully as your Lord, staying in fellowship and under the authority of your local church, casting all of your worry upon the Lord, remaining alert at all times to the wiles of the enemy, and choosing to fight to death if that's what it takes.

"And they overcame him by the blood of the Lamb and by the word of their testimony, and they did not love their lives to the death" (Rev. 12:11). Make that your goal, your top priority. Write it on your heart and on your mind. Make it your heart's desire.

Finally, remember the verses that come before and after that great statement from Revelation 12:

"Then I heard a loud voice saying in heaven, 'Now salvation, and strength, and the kingdom of our God, and the power of His Christ, have come, for the accuser of our brethren, who accused them before our God day and night, has been cast down...Therefore rejoice, O heavens, and you who dwell in them!' " (vv. 10, 12).

Praise God, it is our destiny to win. It is our destiny to be victorious with Christ Jesus. It is our destiny to receive the fullness of the kingdom of God—but only if we're willing and prepared to take what is rightfully ours from the clutches of the enemy.

I challenge you today:

Be God's warrior in this hour!